# THE FOREST IS THE TREE

# THE FOREST IS THE TREE

*Three big reasons to pay attention to this moment*

MICHAEL MARVOSH

WENDINGWAY
BOOKS

This book is not intended as a substitute for the medical advice of physicians. The reader should regularly consult a physician in matters relating to his/her health and mental health, particularly with respect to any symptoms that may require diagnosis or medical attention.

Identifiers

Paperback 979-8-9863547-0-5

eBook 979-8-9863547-1-2

Audio 979-8-9863547-2-9

*To Dad, who taught me to notice the world around me.*
*And to Mom, who taught me to notice the world inside me.*

# CONTENTS

# How to Use This Book

The following icons are meant to be a prompt for action. To get the most out of your reading, be sure to take the opportunity to act.

Pause and Breathe

---

Check In With Yourself

---

Conclusion

---

Long Break - Pay Attention

# CHAPTER ONE

# WELCOME AND INTRODUCTION

HI THERE. WELCOME TO THIS BOOK. I'VE TRIED VERY HARD, FOR A LONG time, to write this for you. It's been quite difficult, but I hope I've succeeded. Well, obviously I've succeeded. You're holding the book in your hands. But as I write these words, I haven't succeeded yet, have I? I could still give up, or even die, before I finish.

Is this a strange way to start a book? Most books don't offer a welcome at the beginning, as if you are visiting their author's home, do they? (Not to mention a bit of self-conscious reflection.) But this is a different kind of book. As you are reading it, it's important that you try to see a very ordinary sort of thing, which we sometimes read books to try to forget. It's that *you are here*. And in order to remind you that you are here, I, as the author, need to show you that I am here, too.

Well. Sometimes, anyway. There will definitely be times when I try to make an argument or explain the way I understand something. Inevitably I get carried away and disappear behind the words. And I hope that you find those parts of the book every bit as interesting as the rest. I will continue to try to call you back, though. Call you back to an awareness of yourself. Perhaps from time to time you could even remember to come back without my having to call. It's important that you know how to do this thing. To be present. To exist, fully, in this moment. Because I believe you're more important than you realize.

Anyway, let's forget about this for a moment. As your host, allow me to tell you a little about myself. Once again, it probably won't be in the usual fashion. Rather than tell you about who I am, I'm going to try to tell you about what I want.

————

## A GREAT CONVERSATION

If I were to try to articulate what I want more than anything else, it would be to reach my arms wide and eat the world, to thereby understand it. I want to know everything, the *why* and *what* of it. It seems to me that life is this peculiar thing where I've been plopped down in the middle of a great mystery called reality, provided with scant few answers about what the heck is going on here, then left more or less to my own devices for a few years until, one day, I inevitably die. What the heck IS going on here? What should I do? Why is all this happening?

No, scratch that last one. The question doesn't need complicating qualifications. I just want to know *why*! Why? Why anything? Why *everything*?

At one point in our lives, I think each of us was the earnest little child, incessantly asking questions like this:

"Why is the sky blue?"

And our parents, diligently trying to prepare us for a career in STEM, answer:

"Because the atmosphere scatters the light."

"Why does the ammos... (little us struggles with the big word) ammosfear scatter the light?"

"Because light bends when it passes through a medium."

"Why?"

"Something to do with waves and particles."

"What are those?"

...

"Oh, look! An ice cream shop!"

Inevitably, we reach the limit of our parents' knowledge before we reach the limit of our curiosity. Well, at least that was true for me. Still today, as a reasonably intelligent adult, the question echoes, constantly, in the chambers of my mind. Why light? Why gravity? Why life? Why death? Why *me*?

I don't know if every person is obsessed with these questions the way I am. I suspect not. I have met plenty of people who don't seem overly concerned with the answers—and plenty others who think they've already found them. Though so far all the answers I've heard seem to me to have simply kicked the can a little further down the road, ready for another "why."

But there are at least enough people obsessed with these questions that, when you look at history in a particular way, you can see the thread of a Great Conversation that has been happening, certainly since writing was invented, but probably going back to when we first became human, and perhaps even beyond that. Perhaps to the origin of life itself, or even the beginning of the universe. The topic of this Conversation is exactly what I'm trying, fumblingly perhaps, to point at here. It's about what it means to be human, how we ought to behave, and why we—or anything—are here in the first place. On a deeper level, I think the Conversation is trying to answer a question that cannot be articulated in words, one I've only ever gotten glimpses of.

I suspect that you, too, may have caught glimpses of the question at one time or another in your life. If you haven't, I hope you find one or two such glimpses in these pages.

One reason I'm writing this book is because I think I've found some answers to this question. Or should I say these questions? Bah, the distinction starts to blur, as if I have existential astigmatism. It's so hard to mentally hold onto these things which can't be expressed using language. Oh well, nothing to do for it but to keep going. I was talking about having found some answers.

Not final answers, by any means, but ones that I, at least—a nonreligious intellectual skeptic—can accept, and which feel like a firm existential foundation from which to look out at reality and continue to ask more questions. So I would like to share those answers with you, in the hopes that they will help you. Or at least in the hopes that you will be able to take them further than I have.

The other reason I am writing this book is in response to what feels like the fraying social fabric of my time. The human world seems increasingly polarized, as if we trust our neighbors, friends, and even family less than ever. This is a disturbing and frightening feeling. This book is my attempt to do something about it.

So, welcome to my contribution to the Great Conversation, another thread in the great tapestry of human thought—one that I hope will also serve in some small way to hold us together through these trying times. Thanks for being here.

————

## READ AT YOUR OWN PACE

A quick note about reading this book:

In our lives, conversations don't happen all at once. They are spread across multiple meetings, sometimes over the course of days, sometimes of years. A lifelong relationship (like a marriage or with your parents or siblings) is, in a way, a conversation that never ends, but is only interrupted by death.

These kinds of extended conversations change us. We

exchange experiences, ideas, and reflections with other people, then we separate for a time to gather more experiences and ideas and reflect on them. Inevitably, like a comet falling toward the sun or a river running downhill to the ocean, we are drawn back to the people who have changed us, and we once again engage them in conversation. This is a great gift of being human. We have access to the minds of other people. In a very real way, we are a collective. We are never truly alone. Our thoughts are filled with the thoughts of others—and though we can't see it in the same way, their thoughts are filled with our own.

Conversations take time, because change takes time. Too much change too quickly and we get overwhelmed and are forced to close ourselves off to the experiences, ideas, and reflections of those we are in conversation with. We stop listening because we can't incorporate all that experience into ourselves. We're all familiar with this feeling, the feeling of *stop! Enough! Slow down and let me sort through all this!* It's the same feeling I imagine children must have when they throw a tantrum. Perhaps we adults would scream, too, were it socially acceptable. Reality just throws so much at us sometimes.

I don't want you to close yourself off, so I encourage you to take this book as slowly as you need to. I have included frequent section breaks, which I hope will remind you to set the book down and think deeply about how the ideas we just discussed fit in with your experience of life—or don't, as the case may be.

————

## EXPECT DISCOMFORT; EXPECT TO BE CHALLENGED

Earlier I mentioned that I think I've found some answers to the Big Questions of the Great Conversation. Specifically, there are three. For reasons of clarity, I call them Big Ideas #1, #2, and #3.

We will get to them before too long, but before we do I want to make sure that we have some common vocabulary to use to talk about them. The next few sections, therefore, will be like packing our bags with the little ideas that will help us talk about the three Big Ideas I'll be proposing.

Something to be aware of before we begin:

These next few sections, as well as other parts of the book, may feel a bit pedantic to you. This is the way I feel about a great deal of philosophy I have read over the years. Must we really go so far down into the weeds about obvious things like the nature of truth and whether human beings have free will?

Somewhat to my chagrin, I have discovered while writing this book that the answer is, "unfortunately, sometimes we must." I don't like being very far down in the weeds, and I try to avoid it whenever possible, but this is what I've learned: our tools of language and reason are in many ways inadequate for dealing with the complexity of reality. Discussing the nature of everything is like trying to dig a hole to the center of the earth with a spoon. We will inevitably fail to understand everything. Nevertheless, I believe there is value in trying (a belief that will become clearer in Big Idea #3 toward the end of the book). What I hope is that you will work through these arguments with me. That you will pay close Attention and try to follow along. Much as I might wish I could, I cannot reach into your head and create understanding there. You must wrestle your own understanding out of your experience—and reading this book is now a part of your experience.

On the other hand, perhaps you are quite comfortable in your intellect—and thus also comfortable with these kinds of highly detailed arguments. If so, I have some bad news for you as well. Our intellects are only a small part of what we are as human beings. If our goal is to understand more about our existence, then we need to take in information in multiple ways. One of the most important sources of information about ourselves and our surroundings is our emotions. Therefore, some parts of this book will lean strongly into our emotional landscape.

In fact, it's my not-so-secret hope that, whether you're more in touch with your emotional side or your intellectual side, you will feel a little bit of discomfort from time to time while reading this book. Discomfort is a sign that you're paying Attention, that you're changing—or at least that you're noticing some ways in which you might want or need to change. It means you're participating in the conversation. It means you're growing, and that you have a chance of coming out better for it. We human beings love to be comfortable, but life often demands that we change, so it's good to be more comfortable with change. Or at least less uncomfortable with it.

# CHAPTER TWO
# LITTLE IDEAS

## LITTLE IDEA #1: YOUR EXPERIENCE OF NOW

*Hey, you.*

Yes, you. Sitting there, reading this book. Reading these very words, in fact. Take a second to notice this experience. You are not the only person to have read these words. Yet you are the only person experiencing reading them right at this moment, hearing whatever voice it is you hear inside your head.

This experience you're having right now is uniquely yours. There is no one else in your head with you. No one but you has brought your lifetime of experiences to this moment. It's just you. This present moment you are experiencing, along with all those that came before it and all those that will come after, are what make up your life. Those moments, melting seamlessly one into the next into the next, are the basis for everything you think, for everything you believe, for everything you are. And more than that—they are the basis for everything you *are capable* of thinking, everything you *could possibly* believe, and everything you *could potentially* be.

We tend not to pay close Attention to our experience of this present moment. There are lots of reasons for this, most of which are understandable. But this first idea—that, despite all the reasons we avoid it, we ought to pay close Attention to this moment, right now—is actually the most important point in the entire book. Of course, there's a lot of ground for us to cover before it will become clear why it's so important. So, for now, just try to keep this idea close at hand while reading: you are the main character in this book. You're the voice of the narrator, and you're also the audience. Don't forget that, and don't diminish it. It's important. You're important.

Take a moment and just notice.

————

## LITTLE IDEA #2: DEFINITIONS

I am not enthusiastic about definitions. For one thing, they tend toward the sort of down-in-the-weeds kind of thinking I've already expressed dislike for. Defining things with perfect precision is impossible, so ornery people can always respond by demanding more precise definitions. It's a downward spiral, and sometimes I suspect the only way to avoid it is to avoid definitions entirely by just pointing at things in the real world. After all, the whole point of definitions is to give us confidence that we're talking about the same thing.

The problem is that we often mistake the definition for the thing we're talking about. That, of course, is wrong. Definitions are only ever pointers. We can argue all day about whether or not the Nile delta is part of the ocean or the river, but when you stand next to someone and show them the thing you want to talk about, it's much harder to misunderstand.

So you'll see that when I try to define things, I will try to get you to connect with an experience you've had (like from idea #1 earlier). The words I use are less important than you doing the work in your head of trying to understand. And understanding is connecting what I'm saying with experiences that you've had. It's not just about reading words.

Here, let's practice with...

———

## LITTLE IDEA #3: BELIEF

Part of the origin of this book is my own personal journey from religious belief to unbelief and back to what I now see as nonreligious belief. Now, when I say belief, I'm not talking about faith. Faith is, as the Christian Bible states, "assurance about what we do not see." Belief is different. Belief is based on our experience.

I do not think any religion is true. But I do think *something* is true, and I think religions are trying to point at it. I just think that, for the most part, they're getting confused. The distinction between faith and belief might be a big part of it. I myself have little, if any, faith. But I've come to realize I have a great deal of belief. What's more, I think *everyone* has a great deal of belief. I think it's a necessary part of being human. (2.1)

The challenge I have when talking about belief is that I think the term is almost always used incorrectly. When most people talk about belief, I think they're talking about *what they think*. About their opinions. And opinions are thoughts.

---

2.1 So, if you consider yourself to be religious, I don't think that's a problem. Faith and belief are not necessarily at odds. Besides, as far as I can tell, religion has always been about trying to figure out what's true. And that's my goal, as well. So there's room for our disagreement here, because we're trying to get to the same place: truth. If we disagree, it's only because we have a difference of opinion on how to get there. On the other hand, if you consider yourself to be nonreligious, well, chances are you and I also see things differently. Because while I think science is one of the most powerful tools humanity has in order to figure out what's true, I also think it's impossible that we will succeed. In other words, I believe there is a mystery within reality that we will never solve, no matter how far we advance in science. By all means, we should continue to do science. At the same time, we should try to avoid the hubris of thinking that we know, well... much of anything at all. Looking back even on our scientific discoveries of the last several hundred years, the one thing they've almost all had in common is that they've turned out to be flawed, if not downright wrong. Why should today's theories be any different?

In my view, beliefs are not thoughts. Not exactly. No, beliefs are deeper than thoughts. Beliefs cannot be expressed in words. They're simply feelings we have: expectations based on our direct experience of the world.

For example, you believe in gravity. You believe that when you take a step, your foot will stick to the ground. You cannot believe otherwise, because your experience tells you this directly. Every step you have ever taken has been consistent when looked at from the perspective of there being gravity. Your belief in gravity is a deeper thing than saying, "I believe in gravity." You can easily see this because were you to say, "I do not believe in gravity," that would be a blatant lie, and everyone would know it. You are incapable of disbelieving in gravity, because your experience of being has so thoroughly taught you that gravity is a true expression of reality.

Beliefs, then, are the way we have learned to see the world, based on our experience. They are like the cognitive equivalent of our eyes. We use our eyes to see, but for the most part we aren't aware of them. In similar fashion, we use our beliefs to perceive the world, but for the most part we aren't aware of our beliefs.

This is a difficult thing to describe, so let's look at another example. As I write this sentence, my coffee mug sits near my right hand. I just took a sip. Yum. I can try to capture all the beliefs I just exercised and render them here in words. I'll almost certainly miss a bunch of them, but I hope the exercise will still prove valuable. I believe that coffee is safe to drink. I believe I enjoy it. I believe it will taste good. I believe the next sip I take will taste the same as the last one. I believe mugs are for holding coffee—or at least that they do a good enough job of it. I believe this particular mug was made for me by my wife's cousin, as a wedding gift to us. I believe in my wife's family. I believe in my wife. I believe all of them love me and want the best for me and part of their expressing that love is in making me mugs I can use to enjoy coffee in the mornings.

So, beliefs are prelingual things we think beneath our thoughts. They come from our experiences. We cannot control them, because the experiential evidence we've received that they are true is overwhelming. I cannot disbelieve in this mug of coffee and what it means to me anymore than I can disbelieve in gravity, or my own existence.

Pause for a moment and reflect on this definition. Think about your own beliefs in this context. Let them sink in. Don't just acknowledge the definition with your language-using brain. Try to notice the experience of your beliefs.

Do you see, by the way, how we're rolling each of these definitions up into one another? All our mental tools are nested and interdependent. It's part of what makes them difficult to talk about, which makes them difficult to agree on. Some people think this next one, doubt, is a bad thing. Perhaps you are one of these people. They/you think doubt is the result of a lack of faith. I disagree, as you will find. Read on.

————

## LITTLE IDEA #4: DOUBT

Now, there is one very useful type of belief we call *doubt*. It might seem strange to call doubt a type of belief since we generally use the term to mean the opposite of belief. But since, given my definition of belief, we are helplessly in its grip, we cannot stop believing anymore than we can stop seeing—and why should we want to? Doubting gravity, for example, would have us all treading so carefully that we'd never get anywhere. But oftentimes reality delivers us experiences that aren't so consistent, or that seem impossible. We're all familiar with optical illusions, for example. Doubt is the belief that we should double-check our perceptions to verify that they're accurate. Doubt is the belief that makes us think, "wait, did that really just happen?" Doubt is a thing we use to render our experiences into better mental representations of the world. And generating mental representations is also what belief is for. So doubt seems likely to be a kind of belief.

If we simply believed everything we perceived, we would often be fooled by the many illusions in reality. Well, to be more precise, the illusions aren't inherent to reality; they're caused by our limited perspective (more on perspective later). Though, to be fair, perspective, too, is inherent to reality... but that line of thinking has us headed for an infinite regress of subjectivity. I think subjectivity exists, but I don't think it's bottomless...

Well, this got mind-numbing rather quickly. You see the tangled nature of being down in the weeds, like I mentioned before. Let's pull up now: the point is that over the course of our lives we have been fooled by enough illusions that we also believe we should doubt.

Doubt is the belief tool we use to validate our other beliefs. It is one of the foundational beliefs of that very useful method we call science. When we doubt, we try to verify. We look at something again and again, from different perspectives, using different tools, different senses. The more ways we verify something, the higher our degree of confidence that it is what it seems to be. The stronger our belief in it.

Doubt is, in this way, the engine of belief. Without doubt, we couldn't have much confidence in our beliefs.

———

## LITTLE IDEA #5: DOGMA

Dogma is a word normally associated with religion, but I don't think it should be. After all, religion is a creation of human beings. So if we can apply the word dogma to religion, we ought to be able to apply it to other things we have created. Dogma isn't a religious thing; it's a human thing.

It would be easy to say that dogma is belief run rampant. I don't think that's quite true, though. Rather, dogma *looks* like belief run rampant. Dogma, as we normally encounter it and think about it, is when someone is so certain of what they *think*, that no amount of evidence to the contrary will convince them otherwise. Dogma is certainty, and I think certainty is always unwarranted—or at least almost always.

One helpful way to distinguish dogma from belief is that—at least in the way I'm talking about the two things here—beliefs are unstated and generally unconscious things. We don't think about our belief in gravity, and we wouldn't think to articulate a creed or manifesto about our belief in gravity. No, gravity is self-evident. That's why we believe in it.

On the other hand, dogma, while it may resemble belief, is not belief. Dogma is thoughts. Notice two paragraphs earlier how I use the word *think* instead of *believe* to refer to dogma. Dogma is always a complex narrative, full of words and justifications and defenses, all aimed at wiggling itself around the fact that reality doesn't actually comport with the dogma's view of the way reality is. We're all familiar with religious dogma: with fantastical stories of miraculous healings, transmutation of one substance into another, water bursting forth from a rock on command, the splitting of the moon and the Red Sea, and of people rising to life after days in the grave—all examples of things we don't observe in reality these days. But, as I said, dogma isn't just a religious thing; it's a human thing.

An example of nonreligious dogma would be thinking that

the earth is flat. We have all kinds of evidence, including not just the word of trusted scientists and mathematicians, but also photographs and videos, that show us renderings of the round earth. To continue to think the earth is flat in the face of all that evidence is very strange. That strangeness is a sign that you've encountered dogma, and it helps us see why dogma is something other than just a very strong belief: because in order for someone to think something that is so obviously contrary to their experience, something else must be going on inside them —something that is preventing them from thinking or perceiving clearly. I think that thing is usually fear, but it might be other things. In the case of flat-earthers, it might be a desire to be seen as quirky and different. Or perhaps a deep mistrust of others?

Consider how I said that we use our beliefs to perceive like we use our eyes to see. Now, imagine losing your eyes—losing your vision. That would be difficult and frightening, wouldn't it?

It is no less difficult and frightening to imagine losing our deepest beliefs. Without them, we would have a much more difficult time navigating our inner world of thoughts.

The unfortunate situation we're in, though, is that the work our eyes do is much easier and more consistent than the work our beliefs do. The physical world looks mostly the same from moment to moment. Most objects' appearances don't change much. Every morning when I wake up, I am greeted by the same brown table. But ideas are complex and ephemeral. When we think what seems to be the same thought two days in a row, is it really the same thought? When I tell my wife, "I love you," do I really mean the same thing every day?

Things I experienced during my upbringing have given me a dogma about loving my wife. Things like my family, my culture, and the training of the religious tradition I was raised with. I am *supposed* to love my wife. But relationships are complex, and in all honesty I feel differently about my wife every day. Those feelings are in part a response to events in my life, in part a response to events that have happened to both her and me, in part a response to... who knows what? Feelings aren't always completely comprehensible. If on some particular day I feel rather annoyed with my wife, my dogmatic idea that I'm *supposed* to love her could easily interfere with my awareness of the truth: that I'm irritated.

Were I religious, the word I'd use for failing to be loving would be *sinful*. And I certainly don't want to be sinful. Better to avoid looking at the truth than to admit to myself that I'm sinful. But avoiding the truth is always a bad thing. And dogma is very good at drawing our Attention away from our own experience, in the moment, of what's true. Because dogma tells us what's *supposed* to be, rather than what *is*.

So you can see it's the same whether or not you're religious. To children, dogma feels like rules and regulations. When adults scold children for behaving badly, they are communicating their dogmas, and children often feel that burning sense of shame you're probably familiar with (I know I am).

It's a little different in adults, though. In adults, I think dogma becomes like the defensive wall we build around our beliefs so that we don't have to feel shameful, lost, and confused when our beliefs turn out not to be true. Instead, when we start to get evidence that our beliefs are wrong, dogma makes us feel justified in getting self-righteous, indignant, and aggressive. Dogma whispers soothingly to us that we can't be wrong, so *they* (whoever "they" are in this case, whether people or groups or ideas) must be wrong. And if they are wrong, they are bad, and if they are bad, then it's acceptable for us to mistreat them however we wish. Dogma makes us attack instead of paying Attention to what's going on inside us and around us.

The frightening and disturbing side effect of extreme dogma is that no amount of reality can shake it. A person caught in the throes of dogma is like a wild animal. There's no reasoning with them. They're unable to see reality for what it is, because their fear is preventing them from forming the necessary new beliefs to do so.

The other frightening thing about dogma is that we are all susceptible to it. It's in all of us. Even if we get self-righteous about how nondogmatic we are, that very self-righteousness becomes a kind of dogma.

Hey. Just checking in. How are you doing? When I reread my book, I sometimes notice around this point that I've started to go a little mentally numb. This is hard stuff. It's like lifting weights with your brain. Except that when you lift too much, you just end up being unable to lift more, whereas when you think too much, you end up scanning each line of words without comprehending any of them. You know the feeling.

Take a break if you need to. This is a good spot to do so. We're halfway through our packing list of ideas.

———

LITTLE IDEA #6: SKEPTICISM

Recall that doubt is a kind of belief that helps us generate new beliefs. In similar fashion, skepticism is a philosophical stance we can take toward reality—and one that helps us minimize the dogma in us.

Skepticism is simply keeping top of mind that our current perspective on things is not the only perspective. A skeptic values a close examination of things from many different angles, compares all those views against one another, and tries to choose the most comprehensive view—or the one with the fewest bad outcomes.

Skepticism is, for example, what allowed Copernicus to figure out that the earth revolves around the sun. He was quite familiar with the belief of his time that the sun goes around the earth. After all, when you look up at the sky, it definitely *looks* like the sun goes around us. But he was skeptical, and his skepticism helped him notice some inconsistencies having to do with inertia and momentum, the erratic movements of the planets, and the fact that the sun didn't take quite the same path through the sky every day, but oscillated higher and lower above the horizon over the course of the year—a fact not easily explained if the sun revolves around the earth.

Copernicus' skepticism butted up against the dogma of his day—especially that of the prevailing power, the Catholic Church. And this kind of conflict is common throughout history. Skepticism and dogma would seem naturally to fall at odds with one another, as they value different things. Dogma values being right, which often ends up demanding blind faith (as opposed to belief), while skepticism values questioning things.

But skepticism, too, can go too far. It is a philosophy that, given too much leash, can eat its own tail.

Because what if we question everything? What if we question our ability to question? What if we question what things look like to us? What if we question our own existence?

At some point our incessant questions begin to undo the fabric of our lives. We might become liable to no longer be sure if we love our families, if our lives have purpose, or if we ought to treat each other with kindness and empathy instead of disdain and violence.

So just like doubt is a kind of belief, skepticism—the very best tool we have of preventing ourselves from becoming dogmatic—also turns out to be a kind of dogma. A way of looking at the world that we can get so comfortable with that we run the risk of starting to think it's the way the world actually is. Too much skepticism is a juggernaut on a direct path to nihilism. And nihilism is, for many people, a very dangerous philosophy.

I consider myself to be a skeptic. I used to be an even stronger skeptic, until I started to notice myself becoming a little more nihilistic than I wanted to be. I'll share some of that journey with you later in the book.

Nihilism is the idea that our lives are meaningless, that the existence of anything is meaningless, that the entire universe is a meaningless accident caused by accidental laws of physics in this particular reality (if reality is even a meaningful distinction). This idea is dangerous. Like a fire, or a gun. Not evil, by any means. Simply a tool capable of doing great damage. People who fall too far into skepticism can become hopeless. Hopelessness, like a burn or a bullet wound, is an acute kind of pain. And pain, when resisted or untended, turns to suffering.

So let's talk a bit about suffering. We must come to our definition through pain, of course.

———

## LITTLE IDEA #7: SUFFERING

Pain is simply our body's response to damage. Stub a toe on the coffee table and you feel pain. It's your brain's way of trying to get you to take a slightly different path through the living room next time. But we also feel pain in response to nonphysical stimuli. Children who get excluded from a game of tag feel intense emotional pain—and for precisely the same reason as a stubbed toe. Their brains know that being a part of the group is good for survival. Being ostracized and alone is dangerous. So, when we get excluded, our brains send the signal, interpreted as pain, that we should try to fit in. It's very similar to safely navigating a path through your living room, avoiding all coffee table legs.

Pain is a good thing. We may not always like it (which is kind of the point), but it is valuable information about what parts of reality are safe, and what parts are dangerous. Those parts can be physical (coffee table legs, heights, spiders), emotional (isolation, rejection, failure), mental (misinformation, misunderstanding), or spiritual (mortality salience, meaninglessness, hopelessness).

Suffering, however, is different than pain. Suffering is something more. Yes, pain is always present when we suffer, but suffering is a special kind of agony, a deep sense of *wrongness*. It is that feeling that, if we could express it in words, might go something like, "this thing that is happening right now should *not* be happening!" Like every fiber of your being is straining for some other outcome than the one currently being forced upon you. It is a feeling of powerlessness, of impotence, this reminder of our weakness and insignificance, that for a few moments (which seem to drag on forever) rips away the facade of control we like to think we have over our lives.

I think it's important to keep that experiential definition close at hand as we think about suffering. But a good shorthand might be something like this: *suffering is pain plus resistance.*

Yes, whether it's a small suffering, like spilling something and making a mess when you were already in a hurry or a big suffering like the loss of a loved one, the suffering only ends when we accept what *is* instead of longing for what *was* or what *might have been*. In cases of great suffering, we often need to go through a grieving process to get to that acceptance, but the fact remains: as soon as we stop resisting, the suffering is lessened. Pain is something that happens. Suffering is something we *do* in response to pain. But it is by no means a *necessary* response.

Now, to hook this up to an earlier idea: what is dogma but a kind of resistance? A resistance to seeing reality as it is, instead choosing to cling to what we would prefer it to be? So dogma inevitably leads to suffering.

There is a lot of suffering in the world. A lot. You know it. I know it. Every human being, no matter how prosperous, is familiar with it. We all suffer, and for many reasons. One of those reasons is because we are dogmatic.

Yes, we bring much of our suffering on ourselves. Perhaps all of it. What's worse, we all export far too much suffering to other people. Part of my hope in writing this book is to help you learn to see some of the ways you are suffering, so that you may tend to those wounds. As you do, I think you will find that, with less suffering in you, you export less to other people. In this simple way, we ease the whole world's suffering. By starting with ourselves.

Recall that we came to this section through skepticism, and that I myself am rather skeptical (either by nature or by habit). I thought I was using skepticism to avoid the suffering that dogma had inflicted on me when I was young. But I have come to see that skepticism itself became a kind of dogma for me. So, while I was no longer suffering from the cognitive dissonance of a faith that told me the world worked in ways my experience and common sense told me it couldn't possibly work, I had simply exchanged that suffering for one of hopelessness and meaninglessness. I was deeply unhappy, and my experience taught me that there was no solace in belief, and none in doubt.

So it seems there is suffering on either side of any given philosophy.

At the same time that I was wrestling through these thoughts, I was coming of age in a world increasingly riven by conflict.

―――――

## LITTLE IDEA #8: CONFLICT

When we observe closely, we notice that suffering only arises where there is pain, but it does not always arise when there is pain. Sometimes wounds are healed well, with little to no suffering. This observation suggests to us that there is at least one way we can respond to pain that does not involve suffering.

To see this, let's look at where wounds come from: conflict.

At its broadest, conflict is when forces collide. Imagine, for instance, a rock smashing into a glass bottle, or two pool balls careening off one another. In fact, we've already had an example of this: the stubbed toe on the coffee table.

We can see that conflict—collisions between forces—causes damage, and always to the smaller, softer, or more fragile of the objects: the toe instead of the coffee table, the bottle instead of the rock. But, looking closer, we see that conflict doesn't *have* to cause damage, as in the case with the pool balls.

What conflict *does* always cause is *change*. The bottle or toe, when colliding with the bigger object, is shattered. The trajectory of both pool balls is altered. Change always occurs after a collision. What does not necessarily occur is that the change be violent or destructive.

Of course, I use examples of physical objects here only to give an easy point of comparison. Indeed, the forces that drive conflict are most obviously imbued in objects like rocks and toes and pool balls, but not necessarily. What I am really talking about here is human conflict.

Remember our other example from before: the excluded child on the playground. In this case, the will of the group of children to exclude overpowers and crushes the will of the one child to be included. Will, too, is a force. It seeks to shape the world, and when it collides with a will it perceives to be in opposition to its desires, that is a collision every bit as real as a rock smashing into a bottle. It's just harder to notice as being a collision between forces.

Dogma, which we discussed earlier, is an expression of will. It is a carefully constructed view—a particularly inflexible one—of the way the world is, and it wants to be right. It wants to be right so badly that it will dismiss evidence to the contrary, then try to change evidence to the contrary, or even, failing that, to attack and destroy evidence to the contrary. Dogma has decided itself to be a rock, and it goes about looking for bottles to smash. But there is always a bigger rock. So dogma is no guarantee of being right. It is, tragically, only a guarantee of conflict, pain, and eventually, suffering.

We human beings are in the unfortunate position of being unable to exist without belief. We must believe in order to perceive. But our beliefs can only ever come from our experience, and our experience is inseparable from our perspective within reality. But what we experience and perceive are not reality itself.

Reality itself is big, and always changing. We, with our limited beliefs and perceptions, are therefore trapped between our little view and the unlimited nature of reality. On the one hand, we want our beliefs to be true enough to keep us alive and thriving, and so we build them up and reinforce them into dogmas. On the other hand, reality is always more complicated than we can know, and it's always changing, so our beliefs and dogmas are constantly being eroded by the continued experience of the very existence they afford us. They will inevitably be eroded until they either collapse or we abandon them.

This is the conflict inherent in being human. There is no escaping it. It is the consequence of being limited in what appears to be an unlimited reality.

Our choice, of course, is to construct either brittle beliefs (like dogmas) and defend them until they shatter; or expansive, flexible beliefs, which are able to flow around the changes in reality and the new things we learn about it every day.

Conflict may be inevitable, but we have the ability to respond to it in many different ways. I think we should try to choose ways that minimize suffering.

————

## LITTLE IDEA #9: SUFFERING THROUGHOUT THE AGES, IN MY WORLD AND YOURS

I do not know when you are reading this book. These words are the disembodied voice of the author as he was at a certain point in the past. It feels a bit strange even to use the word "I" to refer to myself in this book. Of course, I do it all the time. It's convenient. It helps you relate to me. And, in a way, you are having a conversation with me right now—or at least with a past version of me.

The point is, well... let's say instead that the *points* are two: The first is that I am/was writing this book within the context of a certain historical milieu. There are things happening in the world, and the thoughts I share in this book are inevitably a response to my current events—at least in part. The second point is that you are in the same situation as I am/was. You, too, exist in a certain historical milieu. You have an experience of being, of being alive, of being human, that is different than mine in its particulars, but the same as mine in general. Things are/were happening in my life and my world, and I am/was responding to them. Writing this book is/was part of my response. In exactly the same way, things are happening in your life and your world, and you are responding to them. Reading this book is part of your response. These two points, mine and yours, are coming together in this book. Thus two points, at least for a time and from a certain perspective, become one.

But I digress. I was talking about conflict, and about current events at the time I am/was writing this. So, grant me a moment to talk to my readers who are living close to this point in time, and, if you are one of my readers far in the future, stay the course and you will soon see how this relates to you.

It feels like the human world today is falling apart. Fracturing, disintegrating, dissolving. These and similar words all feel appropriate at one time or another. There is a growing divide between the political left and right, between religious conservatives and progressives, between humanity and the environment, between the rich and the poor. People are being killed—sometimes in broad daylight—because of the color of their skin, the content of their beliefs, or the country they happen to have been born in. People are being killed for going to church, school, protests, concerts, and parades. I might cynically say that symbols of capitalism are still safe, but no: people are being killed at shopping malls and movie theaters, too. It feels like violence is escalating. Statistics tell us it isn't, but the media tells us it is. We hear stories every day about some new terrible thing someone has done to someone else. Police continue the long and horrific tradition of mistreating—or outright murdering—people with dark skin. People who protest such things are in turn being gunned down in the streets. Was it because their protest grew violent? Some think yes, others think no. Sometimes the people who pulled the trigger, police and civilians alike, are getting away with no consequences, claiming they acted in self-defense. Opinions seem split on whether or not this is justice—and the more split the opinions, the stronger they become. No one can convince anyone of anything anymore. It's just a deepening of the trenches we dig to defend our opinions. Friendships are ending, family gatherings are erupting in arguments. It's harder and harder to feel safe, wherever we go. The bonds of trust that a civil society rests upon seem increasingly frayed. It feels like we're a hair's breadth from chaos, that one gunshot in the right place at the right time could shatter this whole civilization we've been building for hundreds of years.

There are thousands of examples of ways in which it seems like things are falling apart. In addition to race violence, police brutality, and mass shootings, we have looming climate disaster, conspiracy theories run rampant, political corruption, fundamentalist terrorism (some religious, some not), and the old standbys of famine and disease, all watched over by the rise of the super-rich. In the last two years, all of us have been impacted by the spread of a new coronavirus, COVID-19, which has at times banished us to lonely quarantine within our houses in an attempt to keep ourselves and our loved ones safe. But the success of such strategies has been middling, at best. Close to six million people have died of COVID in the last two years, and no one yet knows how many more will follow. The spread of this virus has driven further wedges between people of different political leanings, religious beliefs, and income levels. Many people think that scientifically produced and tested vaccines are more dangerous than the virus itself. The internet is a breeding ground for its own kind of virus: misinformation. It is becoming more difficult for people to figure out what is true and to act accordingly. Still, we often feel frustrated at people who are duped by such misinformation. I often wonder if I am one of those who has been duped. It seems inevitable that I am, at least in some things.

It is difficult to feel, in such times, that things are not unraveling. That we are not inexorably marching—or being dragged—into the next dark period in human history.

I do not know how these things will turn out. It makes sense to me, however, that if we humans don't find a way to address these problems, then things will get a great deal worse. It has certainly happened before, in, for example, the dark ages of Europe following the end of the Roman empire, or the fall of the USSR.

To my readers in the future, thank you for indulging me. I hope I've painted enough of a picture for you to glimpse what life was like in my time. (I hope that, in your histories, you can see the ways humanity has responded well to the challenges of my day—or at least learned from its mistakes.) Of course, you can see the many ways suffering exists in your time, too. You notice the problems in your life and your world, many of which seem overwhelming. My point is, we're all familiar with suffering. It's part of the cost of existence. Whether you live in my time or another, you know it well. You experience its darkness and pain every day. And, if you're like me, something deep inside you, when you encounter suffering—either your own or that of someone else—cries out, *something is wrong here*. Maybe not always. Maybe there are situations you feel are justified—or which you have to ignore for your own sanity. It's easy, after all, to get crushed under the weight of trying to care about things over which we have no control. But my point is simply this: even if you live in the most ideal utopia humanity has ever managed to create, you are inevitably familiar with suffering. And some part of you—at least that original, deep instruction you received before birth to *SURVIVE!*—longs to do something about it.

Of course, suffering arrives in all kinds of different ways, and it would be callous of me to treat them all equally. My headache is not the same as a divorce after years of marriage, which is not the same as starving during a famine, which is not the same as the death of one's child, which is not the same as a genocide. Whenever we try to talk about possible responses to suffering, we run the risk of dismissing someone's suffering, or trying to analyze it or fix it—all responses which interfere with our ability to empathize with the sufferer. That is one of the most frustrating things about suffering. That it isn't a problem we can solve, but rather a kind of feature of existence. Or at least a feature of being human. More frustratingly, even perfect empathy, if such a thing exists, which is the best imaginable response to someone else's suffering, doesn't really do anything to fix it. Or... does it? An interesting question, but one we must consider later.

I wish I had a solution. Philosophers and prophets have been searching for one for a long time, with no apparent agreement. I do not think I am either philosopher or prophet, and I don't really think I have, or will ever have, a solution. But what I do think I have discovered is a perspective that has helped me lessen the impact of suffering in my own life. I think it can do the same for you, so in the following pages, I'm going to try to describe that perspective. As you will hopefully come to see, it is inevitably the wrong perspective. That might be a funny thing to admit up front, but it will make sense later on. Despite its wrongnesses, I think it's still a pretty good perspective. And if you can combine it with your own, then maybe, just maybe, you will be able to find, if not a solution, at least some answers. Some consolation.

My fear is that we as humanity will not be able to survive unless we can all find a single, foundational belief that we can all agree to share. I hope our conflicts will not be as they have been in the past—like a rock smashing a bottle—but that they will be like two pool balls careening off one another, headed more or less in the same direction and not too much worse for the wear. I hope we are, broadly speaking, working toward finding that shared belief—that common direction. When we find it—if we find it—I think we will have discovered a way to eliminate much of the unnecessary suffering in the world: the suffering we inflict on ourselves and others despite the fact that we ought to know better.

I don't think we'll be able to eliminate all suffering. Much of it happens because of our ignorance and weakness. But I do think we have the ability to make things better. And when we have an ability, I believe we have an obligation to try.

So that's it. That's all we'll pack. I mean, well... of course that's not *it*. There's ever so much more. You can probably see how these ideas are all very big and complex and lean on one another in nuanced and unexpected ways. Figuring out the order to present the ideas in this book has been quite the task. A book has to have things in order, but there's no order to human life. We all learn things in our own time, based on our own experiences. I only hope we can cobble together a similar understanding of this reality we share. And I hope this book helps you in that work, which is the same work of every human being. Another thing we all share.

The next three chapters of the book are three Big Ideas I'm proposing. Three answers to the Big Question. Three foundational perspectives, each very broad yet also very personal, that I hope will enable every person who takes them to connect to a larger sense of being human. They are neither religious nor nonreligious. They are based, first and foremost, in your own experience of being. You can verify them for yourself at any moment, simply by paying Attention.

And, speaking of paying Attention, that is what the final chapter of this book is about. In it, I suggest that paying Attention is the most sensible response to the fact of our existence. That, in a very real way, paying Attention is what human beings exist to do.

———

## PREFACE TO THE BIG IDEAS: A PATH, A WARNING, AND A NOTE

Throughout the writing of this book, I have been keenly aware of a specific tension. I am pulled toward, on the one hand, saying things clearly and directly—of telling you my opinion in as few words as possible, and trying to make it accurate and coherent. On the other hand, I am cognizant of the fact that I cannot inject understanding into you. No, understanding is something you need to assemble for yourself, out of your own experience and reflection. And in order to experience and reflect, we little physical beings must struggle.

I don't know that I have navigated this tension perfectly. In fact, I'm rather certain there is no perfect path. And in any case, we all must follow different paths, because our lives and our experiences of being are all different. Sort of. We'll get into that more in Big Idea #2.

My point here is that I can't simply take you step-by-step through my own journey. You are on your own journey and must take your own steps toward understanding. You are reading this book right now, which means that, at least for a short time, our journeys are indeed overlapping. But still, I won't immediately state things directly because of the one big thing I hope you take away from your reading of this book, the thing which I think might be the work of every human being: that you pay Attention. And if you know precisely where we're going, with too much ease, then there is less reason to pay Attention. But if you're not sure, and you're highly aware of treading this specific ground for the first time, then I suspect you'll bring a greater degree of Attention to this work than you normally might.

Of course, again I realize that I can be too incoherent, too fuzzy, and that I can write too much mumbo jumbo. In my intellectual, rational, skeptical way, I think this is by far the more frustrating failing, so in each case when I am uncertain how direct to be, I have tried to err on the side of clarity. Hence, for example, the packing list we just completed.

Anyway, be aware. There is work to do ahead. Pay Attention.

Finally, I would be remiss if I didn't note that all of this stuff is just my opinions, based on my experience and reasoning. As you read, it will become clear that I think no one can really know what's true. All we can do is compare our experiences in the hopes of developing better descriptions of reality. But it's not the descriptions that are true—only the reality. That being said, I have put a great deal of time and effort into examining my opinions, and I believe they are well-reasoned. If you disagree with any of my conclusions, I hope you will let me know. That is, after all, how we get better. To this end, I've included my contact information at the end of the book.

# CHAPTER THREE

# BIG IDEA #1

"Whereof one cannot speak, thereof one must remain silent."

*— LUDWIG WITTGENSTEIN, ON THE*
*INDESCRIBABLE NATURE OF REALITY*

## INTRODUCTION

THERE IS A COMMON SAYING: DON'T MISS THE FOREST FOR THE TREES. IT is an exhortation to not pay such close Attention to the details of a thing that we miss the beautiful whole.

I have a bad habit of looking at my feet when I walk. It's not such a big deal in the city, as there aren't all that many particularly beautiful vistas to behold. But when I hike in the woods, I often fall into the same habit. And so, rather than walking through a forest, I find myself walking past a root, then a few pinecones, then some dirt, then a fern, then another root. On and on, for thousands of steps, repeating essentially the same scenery over and over. Root, rock, rock, root, dirt, dirt, dirt.

It is only when I look up that I remember why I love to hike in the woods. When I come to a rise, and the forest drops away before me, and I can look out and see the trees blanketing the landscape, off into the mountainous distance, I am quite simply struck dumb. There are no words for the sensation. But, well, we are in the middle of a book here, and books consist only of words, so I'll try to find some that will do, paltry as they may be.

In such a moment of beholding, a moment of pure Attention, the *me* that was just a minute earlier picking his way along a forest trail suddenly disappears, becoming just one more part of this ancient landscape.

I get the feeling that I am simultaneously tiny yet vast, insignificant yet supremely privileged—because I am both a part of the view and the one seeing the view. It's a breathless feeling, as if some primal force of nature reached right down into the depths of me and ripped the air from my lungs. Again, there are no words that fully describe this kind of experience. It just *is*. It's a moment overflowing with *is*-ness.

Yet upon reflection, it occurs to me that this moment of beholding the forest must share something fundamental with the previous moments of picking my way along the path, staring at my feet. They are, after all, both moments in the past. The universe worked equally hard to bring them both into existence. The only difference, if there was one, was that in one moment I was *there*—fully present, participating in the spectacle—while in the other moment I disappeared somewhere—into my head, perhaps—in response to what I perceived to be monotony.

Yes, upon reflection it occurs to me that the one moment is not substantially different than the other. It is *I* who is different. I am no less a part of the landscape while lost on the trail than I am when surveying the vista. A minute spent examining a tree is no different than a minute spent overlooking a forest. So why do I perceive the two experiences as different? Why is the forest considered beautiful, and the tree considered... just a tree?

In the following chapter, I hope to show you why the title of this book is what it is. I hope to show you why I think the forest is the tree, and why our distinction of the two is not as clear as we like to think it is. I hope to show you a different perspective on what's real than the one you are used to. And I hope that this new perspective will help you begin to see a future in which you and the people around you suffer less.

————

## THE IDEA: THERE IS ONLY ONE REALITY, WHICH NOT ONLY CONTAINS EVERYTHING BUT *IS* EVERYTHING

As I watch the steam billow and swirl off my coffee, I wonder how it "knows" to move this way. I'm not necessarily attributing any kind of intelligence to the complex dance I'm observing— certainly not a human kind of intelligence. I think it's really just particles bouncing off one another, caught up in the flows of air they find themselves moving through while simultaneously tugging those flows upward with the energy of their heat. But that does not make it not beautiful.

Well... it doesn't make it not intelligent, either. Indeed, the particles of steam "know" how fast they're moving, they "know" when they bump into another particle, and they "know" when they've escaped to a place where they can dissipate their excess energy and gently merge with the rest of the air in the room— the exact place at which the steam itself dissipates.

I wonder, idly, if I am a thing like one of those particles: an object bouncing through space, spun about by the vicissitudes of chance or fate; or by the social currents through which I drift, some tugged along in my wake. Do I, too, billow and swirl? Are my movements also beautiful?

I also wonder if the steam is like me: trying to live a good life. Wondering if it's doing the right thing. Is it afraid as it leaves its coffee home and rises up, up, up past the increasing millimeters of exposed mug? I take another sip, and its journey is that much farther. Am I the coffee's grim reaper? Is its steam some sort of early warning system against my all-consuming entropic mouth?

Observing the steam rising off my coffee in the half-awake mental space of early morning, I notice something unexpected rising in me: envy. The steam moves with such quiet confidence, never second-guessing itself or circling back to try again. It has something I will never possess: perfect belief. A total conviction that it is what it is, that this is how it ought to move; it never fails to behave in precisely the "correct" way.

Now, I can hear what you may be thinking. *You're anthropomorphizing, Michael.* And you'd be right. Steam isn't like a human, and we should be careful to maintain the distinction. And yet, on the other side of the coin... are we humans like the steam? Do we never behave instinctively, without much, if any, conscious awareness of what we're doing? Are we not, on a deeper level than our minds, physical beings whose bodies must obey the same universal laws as the steam?

The steam moves as if each particle has the energy it has, drifting along in its particular air current. Do we not also interact with the world as if we have ten fingers, eyes that can perceive a certain part of the electromagnetic spectrum, and brains that can process a limited amount of information? Are we not also constrained by the properties of our physical bodies? Are we not caught up in social currents, behaving so often as we do because it is what the other people with whom we are in close proximity are doing? Do we not anthropomorphize ourselves—perhaps even into existence?

And, when we die, do we not slowly dissolve into the earth and air until eventually there remains no trace of our passing? Aren't we, too, just a pattern the universe produces for a time?

There is a well-known story about a group of blind people who hear that an elephant has been brought to town. Curious about this new creature, they agree to encounter it and explore it with their hands, that they may learn what an elephant is like. They approach the elephant from six different angles.

The person whose hands fell on the elephant's ear said, "Ah! An elephant is like a rough fan: flat and thin."

The person whose hands fell on the elephant's leg said, "No, you are wrong. An elephant is like the trunk of a tree: thick, round, and upright."

The person whose hands fell on the elephant's tusk said, "You are both wrong! An elephant is like a mighty spear: long and smooth, with a pointy end."

The person whose hands fell on the elephant's flank said, "You are all wrong! An elephant is like a rock wall: vast, immovable, rough, and dry."

The person whose hands fell on the elephant's tail said, "Fools! An elephant is like a large brush: straight and thin, with a bunch of bristles on the end."

Finally, the person whose hands fell on the elephant's trunk said, "I am the one who is right. An elephant is like a thick snake: long, muscular, and flexible."

The elephant handler arrived to lead the beast away, ears, legs, tusks, flank, tail, trunk, and all. The blind people remained, arguing amongst themselves.

I used to think this was a story about truth. About realizing that the blind people in their bickering (and their blindness) were failing to see the truth the elephant handler knew but quietly walked away with. I thought the moral of the story was that we should just try to be open-minded, to see the whole picture. That we should be slow to jump to the conclusion that we're right and that someone else is wrong—certainly without first walking over and trying to see what things look like from their perspective. You know, "walking a mile in someone else's shoes," and all that.

And that's not exactly wrong. The story is about those things. But I've come to realize that the story of the elephant is also about something more than this. Something more nuanced. And when we take the time and spend the necessary Attention, we can see how important that lesson is in our day-to-day lives.

The lesson, put simply, is this: do not mistake belief for truth.

Recall that our beliefs come from our experiences, and our experiences are bound to a single, quite small, human perspective. When we see the color red, for example, our perception plus our belief plus our understanding of color makes us think, "that is red."

But reality, at that moment, is not thinking, "now I am showing this human the color red." No, reality isn't aware of color. Red isn't something that *exists* in reality. It's simply the way that we perceive certain parts of reality, and we call those parts red.

In the same way, reality is not thinking, "now I am showing these humans an elephant." Reality isn't aware of elephants. Elephants are simply a thing that we perceive as being a certain kind of object within reality.

I can demonstrate this shaky relationship between what we perceive and what actually is the case in reality by revisiting something we touched on in the preceding section about dogma: the shape of the world.

It used to be that a significant number of people thought the world was flat. (As we discussed before, an embarrassing number of people still think so today, which is a wonderful example of how strong a force dogma can be in our lives.) Once we gained a larger perspective, though, by scientifically observing the heavens and measuring the length of shadows on different points of the earth's surface and those kinds of things, people realized that the earth is round. They changed their belief to match what they observed.

But were those round-earth pioneers actually doing anything different than the flat-earthers who came before them? Flat-earthers thought the earth was flat because it *looked flat*. It's not like they were floating in outer space looking down at our blue marble and saying, in complete denial of what they were observing, "yup, that thar's flat." No, their thinking that the earth was flat is completely understandable given their experience, having never gone more than a few miles from the village where they were born.

*In exactly the same way*, we round-earthers are looking at the earth and saying, "yup, that thar's round." We have all kinds of evidence to support this perspective that the flat-earthers didn't have. And yet somehow we have the audacity to say that we're right and they were wrong.

But the *reason* that we say the earth is round is, again, *exactly the same* as the reason those flat-earthers said it was flat: *because it looks like it is*.

This is a profoundly bad reason to believe something. What's to say that at some point in the future when scientists discover, say, extra dimensions, they won't redefine the shape of the earth as a hypersphere? Or that future discoveries about the nature of time reveal to us that the earth's shape is actually some kind of temporal spiral?

Yes, "because it looks like it" is a really bad reason to think something is true. Yet we are in the unfortunate position of it being the best we can do.

This is part of what it means to be human. Our perspective and the beliefs we extract from it are ever so limited. They are far from an accurate representation of reality. For all we know, they might be infinitely distant from an accurate representation of reality. Yet they are all we have. We must rely on our most up-to-date beliefs about the color red, animals like elephants, and the shape of the earth, because to try to do anything else is impossible. We can't see reality for what it actually is—in no small part because we are a part of reality. (Though this isn't, as we will discuss in more detail later, a good reason not to try to see reality more clearly.)

So you see, the story about the elephant isn't a story about some blind people and an elephant. It's not a story about some people being wrong and other people being right, like those dumb flat-earthers and us more enlightened folks, ha ha. No, it's a story about all of us. It's recursive. We are the blind people of the story, thinking of an elephant. We, too, are in the situation where what we are perceiving is not reality in its fullness, but only what this little part of reality looks like to us. We, who are, after all, just another little part of reality.

For as long as philosophy and science have existed—and even before them, religion and spirituality—we human beings have been trying to make sense of this reality in which we find ourselves. We have been trying to gain the larger perspective, to, as it were, see the whole elephant for what it really is.

And yet, as we have built telescopes to look out at the heavens, we have always found something farther away. So we built larger telescopes, and they observed things still farther away. We even imagine building a telescope out past the orbit of Pluto, so far that it uses the gravitational lensing of the sun itself, turning the entire solar system into a telescope. I suspect that in the distant future, if we ever succeed in building this EM Sunlens telescope, we will find more of the same: there's still something farther away. For now, we seem to have hit a wall in that we can't see past the Big Bang. But, well, we've been unable to see past things before, and have eventually figured out a new way of looking. Why should this time be any different? If our repeated experience has taught us anything, it's that the universe goes outward infinitely.

What about the other direction? What if, instead of looking to the large, we look to the small? We find the story is the same. Microscopes allowed us first to see annelids and flatworms in water, cutely dubbed "animalcules" by van Leeuwenhoek. More powerful microscopes allowed us to see bacteria, individual cells. Experiments deduced the structure of molecules, while other experiments eventually revealed the structure of the atom itself. Surely that must be the smallest building block of reality. But no, we went on to discover protons and electrons and neutrons, and from there quarks and gluons, leptons and bosons. These exist in some kind of quantum realm which seems to somehow be the fabric of reality, yet which doesn't follow any of the same rules. There are theories about strings and things still smaller than these quantum particles. (Not that I understand any of this.)

The point is, why should we imagine that there is a limit to how small things can get, either? If we're going to go off our experience of what things look like to us, then it makes sense to take a historical perspective as well. And, looking at the two above histories—that of the large and the small—it seems that any expectation that we will ever find the limits of reality is completely unfounded. No one has ever seen them. Why should we assume that someday someone will?

This is difficult for me to wrestle with, because I highly esteem science and scientists. I think they are, for the most part, brilliant—certainly much smarter than me. And yet, I cannot help but be aware that in a fundamental way they are doing the same thing the rest of us are: looking at reality and describing what they see. And they are in the same situation the rest of us are, too: they are bound to a perspective, and their beliefs shape what they are able to perceive.

Roundabout 1700, an ideological movement rose out of Europe, its ideas closely tied to that of science. Today we call this movement the *Enlightenment*. Its pioneering thinkers, great men like John Locke and Jean-Jacques Rousseau, were interested in many things, but their ideas that took root in the Enlightenment were mainly political and sociological. They thought and wrote about what human beings are, how we ought to treat one another, and right and wrong ways to govern the abstraction we call "the people."

Enlightenment thinkers prided themselves on being more scientifically minded than philosophically minded. They were trying to discover what they called "natural law," which refers to the idea that there are right and wrong answers to the ways human beings ought to live. There remains to this day a great deal of disagreement about whether or not natural law exists, though most conversations have moved on from there.

I won't revisit that conversation with you here, but I do want to give you a general understanding of one of the big ideas of the Enlightenment: that the individual is sovereign. That everyone was—or ought to be—the ruler of their own life. If you and I had been born previous to the popularization of this idea, then we would rarely, if ever, have thought that we should make decisions in our own self-interest. Which now, of course, is how we make decisions every moment of every day. Back then, we would have made decisions in the interest of king and country (or at least that would have been the internal narrative we would have been telling ourselves when making decisions). Prior to the Enlightenment, everyone behaved as if the Sovereign was sovereign (hence the term). But in the years following the Enlightenment, this idea (and others) of the

Enlightenment thinkers slowly spread and gained acceptance. They were taught to children, then taught to those children's children, then when those children grew up to become university professors, they were taught in schools, and later in churches. In this way, these ideas eventually became the generally accepted "way the world is." And now you and I use these ideas to think without even noticing or considering where they came from. All we're aware of doing is thinking. Our minds are filled with the thoughts of people long dead. And, whether or not we do well, the minds of future generations will be filled with our thoughts. Let's work to make those thoughts better. For our descendants.

Today, because there is such widespread unconscious agreement (at least in Western society) that the individual is sovereign, nearly everyone behaves as if it's true. And when enough people act as if something is true, then in a very real way it becomes true. This is called a social construct. It is closely tied to one of the ideas we packed in our bags earlier: belief. Remember that belief comes from experience. We believe in gravity because we experience it. Social constructs are the same. We believe that the individual is sovereign because when we observe other people's behavior, we see them acting that way.

But social constructs are different in one important way from things like gravity. We believe in them because they exist, yes. But, unlike physical phenomena, social constructs exist *because we believe in them.*

This simple idea gives rise to all sorts of complexity, conflict, and suffering in our world today. You are probably familiar with motivational sayings such as, "change your beliefs, change the world." Rational skeptics such as myself tend to roll our eyes at such things, thinking, perhaps, that they are referring to phenomena like gravity. No amount of belief or disbelief in gravity is going to change how it functions. On the other end of the spectrum, dogmatically religious people will scoff at the idea of changing their beliefs, secure in their knowledge that they have already found the truth.

The difficulty here—the tragedy, really—is that it's easy to make mistakes when it comes to belief. The skeptics I mention above are making the mistake of thinking that beliefs only ever proceed from experience. But that's not true, because social constructs also do the opposite. Social constructs *do* change the world. They have done so before, and will do so again. They are the infrastructure of revolutions and breakthroughs of all kinds. All human progress has greatly relied on progressive social constructs.

On the other hand, the dogmatics I mention above are making the mistake of thinking that their beliefs are actual truths. But, as we saw with the story of the elephant, this is simply not what beliefs are. Beliefs are mental representations of reality, not reality itself. In fact, the very same religious traditions that so often cause people to fall into dogma have a word to describe worshiping unchanging ideas instead of a living God. They call it *idolatry*. And that's what I think dogma is: a form of idolatry.

Despite their differences, I suspect the difficulty both these groups have in seeing belief for what it is is the same. It's that our beliefs about the world keep us safe. And so the idea that our beliefs are insufficient, or misplaced, or downright wrong is scary. Terrifying, in fact. Belief is such a deep part of us that most people confuse it with their very identity. They think they *are* their beliefs. So any thought of changing their beliefs means the loss of their very selves. If that's not existentially frightening, then I don't know what is.

Confronting this existential cliff is a big part of what this book is about. It seems to me that if humanity doesn't do a better job of recognizing our beliefs and updating them to match reality (both the reality that is and the parts of it we have created), then we will continue to head down the path toward eventual self-destruction.

There is another idea that runs counter to the Enlightenment idea of the individual-as-sovereign. Despite it being an almost perfectly opposite idea, it has, in the way only the serendipity of language can produce, exactly the same name: enlightenment.

Enlightenment is an old idea. We mostly see it come to us out of Asia—what we often call the East. Another intriguing diametric difference between it and the Enlightenment which came out of Europe—what we often call the West. Enlightenment is difficult—perhaps impossible—to describe. It refers to a certain kind of awareness in the present moment. Well, perhaps not even a certain kind. I think what enlightenment strives for is *total* awareness (though I suspect any practitioner of enlightenment ideas would suggest that such perfect total awareness is impossible). Total awareness of what exists. Of reality. Of what IS. It notices that everything is constantly changing from one moment to the next. It notices that everything is interconnected, moving in infinitely complex patterns. And it also notices that the one doing the noticing is the same as the things it is noticing. It is always changing. It is connected to everything. When a person is in a state of enlightenment, they are keenly aware of the fact that they don't really exist—at least not in the way you and I are used to thinking about our existence. No, enlightened individuals look at the world in a very different way than those of us who are products of Western Enlightenment ways of thinking.

So here we have in front of us two beliefs of the same name, that indicate polar opposite perspectives on the world and arose, in turn, on opposite sides of the globe. The Western Enlightenment tells us the individual is sovereign, while Eastern enlightenment tells us the individual is a kind of illusion. The Western Enlightenment tells us that human progress comes from each individual striving for their own self-benefit, while Eastern enlightenment tells us to simply observe and accept what is.

Is one of these philosophies more based in actual reality, like gravity, while the other is based more in a socially constructed reality? Must we forsake one enlightenment for the other if we desire to succeed in not destroying ourselves? Or can we somehow combine these apparent opposites into a more holistic way of looking at things?

I hope it is the latter. I think it's possible that we can learn this more holistic way of being human. But it will require us to learn some new ways of looking at things, as well as some new methods for utilizing the ways we already look at things.

A big part of this work will have to do with overcoming our confusion between our beliefs and our identity, and with developing our ability to clearly distinguish between the two things. The next chapter, Big Idea #2, looks at that in more detail.

I took us on this little detour through the enlightenments as a demonstration of how our beliefs shape what we are able to perceive, because the question we're trying to answer in this section is about what we are perceiving. What is this reality we find ourselves in, that we see all around us?

As an exercise, let's take an Eastern enlightenment mindset for a moment.

Imagine that you don't exist. That you're magically plucked from this very moment. Or, if that's too difficult, imagine it's 1800 and you aren't born yet, or that it's 2200 and you are more than a century dead. Does reality still exist?

I suspect your answer is "yes." I suspect that's most people's answer. That reality is a thing that exists independently of their perception of it.

Now, imagine that *no one* exists. That no conscious, language-using mind exists or has ever existed anywhere in reality. In such a case, would that reality still exist? (3.1)

This is a more difficult question. Or, at least, it's one I wrestled with for a long while before coming to a conclusion

I think such a reality would still exist—but in the absence of any mind to think "this exists," or anything along those lines, such a reality would be pure undifferentiated experience of being. Perception as we generally experience it is rendered to us through our thinking mind. If there are no thoughts, no words, then perception is quite a different thing.

What would a wordsless reality be like? It would be, simply, unwordsable. Unimaginable.

The weird thing is, *we already live in that reality*. As far as we can tell, this universe hasn't always had thinking minds in it. We've just figured out how to put words to it now that we're here.

But we need to keep in mind that the wordless reality preceded the words. And so our words and the thoughts they encapsulate cannot be reality. They are only indicators—patterns pointing to different parts of reality, struggling to construct still more elaborate patterns. In the same way that gravity pulls hydrogen atoms together until they organize into a flaming ball of helium-generating fusion we call a star, we organize our perceptions into ever more complex thoughts, which

---

3.1 This sort of thought exercise is the same idea beneath the well-worn question, "If a tree falls in the forest and no one is around to hear it, does it make a noise?" In a funny not-completely-coincidental way, this reference to trees and forests echoes the title of this book—and perhaps it gives us an answer to boot. If the forest is the tree, of course the falling tree makes a noise: on the one hand, it changes the forest forever; on the other, it is simply part of a continuum of change that has always been happening. It is, as I am trying to articulate with Big Idea #1, part of everything.

enable more detailed perceptions, which are again organized into thoughts.

When we forget that we, too—including our thinking—are a part of the process of the universe, when we imagine that we are somehow separate from the rest of it, different—perhaps more important—then we have allowed our thinking to fool us. We have fallen under an illusion; the illusion that *we can know what's true*.

But we can't know that. Truth, if it exists, is connected to all the rest of reality by the same substance that makes up reality itself. It's all one truth, all one reality.

I've used these three stories—the story of the steam from my coffee, the story of the elephant, and the story of Enlightenment versus enlightenment—to demonstrate to you the sense of what I'm trying to say, that the forest is the tree. The trouble with what I'm trying to do is that it's impossible. There's no way to make sense of reality. It's just too big for that kind of thing.

I am not trying to say that the distinction between forest and tree is vacuous. Quite the contrary, it is based on our perception of what exists in reality—and our perception is every bit as real as the things we perceive. At the same time, our perception is not reality itself. It's just reality translated through our senses and beliefs. When we observe a forest, we don't really see the individual trees. In the same way, when we observe a tree, we don't really see the individual plant cells. In both cases—no, in ALL cases—we are observing the same reality.

When I was young, I believed Christianity was true. It was the religion I was raised with. When I was in college, I lost my faith in that religion because I noticed several contradictions within its theology. I thought about them, talked to my friends about them, even took them to my religion professors to discuss. No one was able to find anything wrong with what I'd noticed.

And so I abandoned Christianity as nonsense. How could something that was self-contradictory be true? I figured the same was likely the case with any other religion. The idea that one of them has gotten it right while the others have gotten it wrong is simply too terrible to accept. If that's the reality whatever God there is created, then it is only just that I should reject that God.

I turned to science as my way of understanding reality. It helped salve my cognitive dissonance, at least. It's not that science has no contradictions, but that when one is discovered, a great deal of work goes into trying to correct one side or the other of the disagreement. In other words, science updates its dogma in response to new evidence.

But I discovered over time that science left part of me feeling malnourished. It wasn't a part of me I was greatly in touch with. I think it had retreated deep inside me after I lost the faith of my childhood. But it started to express itself again a handful of years ago. It was the part of me that longs for meaning and purpose. The part of me that, after much deliberation, I can only call my spirit. I didn't know what it was at the time of its reawakening. I think I know what it is now, and will discuss that in the next chapter of the book, Big Idea #2.

I felt caught in a trap. Belief systems that gave me a sense of purpose were internally contradictory, and therefore not true; while belief systems that tried their utmost not to be internally contradictory gave me no sense of purpose.

And so I started searching again, for a perspective on reality that would be both internally consistent and meaningful. What I discovered surprised me, both because it was so simple that I wasn't sure how I could have missed it, and because it was so slippery that I couldn't wrap my mind around it.

It's the Big Idea I'm trying so earnestly yet fumblingly to describe in this section of the book. That reality is far too big to make sense, not because it doesn't make sense but because we are so tiny compared to it. No description or system of belief could capture it. No definition could perfectly describe it—not even any individual piece of it.

And it strikes me that this way of looking at my existence—as well as at existence as a whole—is a lot like looking at the forest and the tree. It's all there. I am witness to it, but it doesn't need me to witness it to exist and be true. The small things make up the large things, and the large things are made up of the small things. Everything is interdependent and connected. It's all just one thing. The forest is the tree.

Of course it doesn't make sense. How could it? But if anything is true, it seems like it must be this. It seems like what must be true is... everything. At least everything that exists. If so, then the only sense to be found can only be found in this nonsense.

When I try to hold onto this perspective, I am struck by the fact that the breathless feeling I described when overlooking the forest is, in fact, available to me at every moment. That each minute and second of my life is full of such unimaginable complexity that it boggles the mind. I have the choice to cower in terror of that complexity, or to try to untangle it, or to simply revel in its beauty. By no means do I need to choose the same response every day. And not only are these things true for me, but they are true in exactly the same way for everyone else. It's just that many of us have learned not to notice.

All human conflict is inevitably resolved in one of two ways. The first way we have already discussed: it's like the rock and the bottle. One individual or group overpowers or destroys the other. Boom. Conflict resolved.

The other way for us humans to resolve conflict is to work together to find something we agree on that's deeper and more important to us than the thing we disagree about. If we can do this, then we can work together to move closer to the goal we agree on. Recall the previous example of two pool balls colliding, then imagine them shooting off in the same direction. Disagreement can remain about the best way to achieve the shared goal, but the disagreement is now in service of accomplishing something together, instead of simply becoming senseless conflict.

Big Idea #1—that reality is just one thing we are all a part of —is not just an idea. It's the *biggest possible idea*. If everyone in the world were able to go back to this idea easily and as often as necessary, then we would always have a deeper shared belief to use to resolve our conflicts productively, instead of destructively. If there is a way to eliminate suffering, it seems like it must lie on the other side of this realization.

The funny thing is, I think that each and every one of us used to know how to look at reality in this way. When we were first born, before we learned any words, the only way we had of perceiving what was real was by perceiving. We didn't yet have the tool of language that allowed us to artificially chop up reality into the distinct pieces you and I are able to use to refer to—and argue about—things like forests and trees.

And so I think the spiritual work of all humanity is to try to remember the thing that learning to speak—and from there, eventually to think—caused us to forget: that the forest and the tree are the same. Part of the same thing. As are you and I and everything that is and was and will be. All part of the same reality.

Remembering this big truth will require us to be able to stop thinking from time to time, and just pay Attention to the world around us—and to the world inside us.

Speaking of the world inside us, that brings us to the next Big Idea.

CHAPTER FOUR

# BIG IDEA #2

"Trying to define yourself is like trying to bite your own teeth."

— *ALAN WATTS*

## INTRODUCTION

THE IDEA THAT THE FOREST IS THE TREE IS A DIFFICULT ONE TO HANG onto because our lived experience of forests and trees suggests to us with perfect consistency the fact that forests and trees are quite different things.

In Big Idea #1, I tried to explain why that distinction is, at least in part, a misperception. If we take the small assumption that everything is connected, then we see, in that simultaneously sensible and nonsensical way of reality, that the distinction between forest and tree is both meaningful and meaningless. (Here my mind wonders for a moment if the idea that everything is connected is even an assumption given how much we've learned so far in the 21st century about the nature of the submicroscopic world of atoms and quantum phenomena— but then I get caught up once again in the recursive loop that we can't really know anything for certain—just what things look like to us. I also worry about the modern trend of self-help books like *The Secret*, which talk about magical ideas such as manifesting, and I can't help thinking that they're spreading a misperception about how all this works. Part of me takes umbrage at that because the truth is so important to me and I would like to think that humanity is capable of more than merely thinking that some magical servant—whether God or some inner genie—is going to wave their hand and make everything better when it seems abundantly clear from all the terrible things people around the world and across time have experienced that this is not the case. But another part of me wonders if there really is any difference between that kind of magical thinking and what I'm trying to express in this book. I think there is. If I'm honest, I'm quite sure there is. I just wish I could prove beyond a shadow of a doubt that there is. Alas, I think the best I can do is try to persuade. Okay, that's enough self-indulgence for a while. Back to the idea at hand...) And in a universe where things can be both meaningful and meaningless, what, if anything, can we hold onto?

Oh, wait. At the end of the last chapter I just got done talking about how we need to learn how to think less. And then what do I do? I go and fill up an entire paragraph with some rambling insecurities about whether or not this book is right, or whether I am making the same mistakes as the very books I disagree with, or whether there is any connection between those things. Ack, maybe I am crazy. Well, if I am, I have the same range of possible responses: cower in terror, try to untangle it, or just dance with it. In any case, time will tell.

Let's get back on track.

What happens when we stop thinking? And what can we learn from it? That's what this next chapter of the book is about. We have a tricky task in front of us because our only way of approaching it is a bit self-sabotaging; a book is necessarily a bunch of words, and words require us to think. Can we learn how to not think by doing a whole lot of thinking? Well, we've done the reverse: when we were babies, we learned to think even though we didn't used to be able to do so. Now, as adults, we need to use our thinking to remember how to not think.

Thinking is a tool. We learned to pick it up and use it when we were babies. Many of us got so good at using it that we can no longer put it down—we fear we wouldn't recognize ourselves without it. And that's understandable, in a way. Thinking is a profoundly useful tool, and when we can employ it with maximum dexterity, it makes our lives better. But maximum dexterity also requires us to be able to set a tool down from time to time and use a different tool. That's what we're trying to do in this chapter: use the tool of thinking in order to help us set the tool of thinking down—at least sometimes.

Big Idea #1 was about what reality is. Big Idea #2 is about who *you* are.

———

BIG IDEA #2: THE CORE OF YOUR SELF IS THAT
PART OF YOURSELF WHICH YOU CANNOT
DIRECTLY PERCEIVE; FUNDAMENTALLY, YOU ARE
THAT WHICH PERCEIVES

Used with permission from @strangetrek

I laughed when I first read this comic. I hope you enjoyed it, too.

At the risk of explaining the joke, I'll say that what particularly struck me as funny was how it subverted my expectations. I thought the cat was going to say how it wanted to be like the squirrel, thus completing the circle of irony. But no, silly. Of course a cat would think itself perfect.

I realized the comic would be a great introduction to Big Idea #2 because I use the idea of a cat's experience of being a few times in the pages to come. I think it's a good mirror to help us recognize ourselves.

A cat never gets upset about the fact that it is a cat, as anyone who has ever owned a cat will tell you. Cats might get upset about some things, true. But they never wish they were something else. Every response cats have when they get hungry, or scared, or want attention, is a perfectly authentic response. In other words, cats never fail to behave precisely like cats, and we can assume they never have an experience of being upset about the fact that they are cats.

The same is true of human infants. They never fail to behave exactly like a human baby will. Sure, sometimes people might say something like, "he's not a very good baby," but what they usually mean is, "she cries more often than I wish she did," or, "he doesn't sleep for as long as I want to sleep." But these aren't problems with the baby's behavior. They're just certain people's responses to the baby's behavior. A baby's behavior is always precisely in line with what a baby is.

This sense that we get of animals and infants perfectly fitting into their own skin is, I suspect, what we are referring to when we talk about innocence. Cats are innocent, as are babies and deer and trees and clouds and pretty much all the rest of what we usually call "the natural world."

But consider a slightly older child, making a statement like, "when I grow up I want to be a dragon." We might chuckle at the naivete of a statement like this and confuse that naivete with innocence, but they are not the same thing. This dreaming child is inevitably sowing the seeds of its own future discontent. It has begun figuring out how to be a storytelling adult. Because, eventually, children are no longer like cats, are they? Somewhere along the line they figure out how to suffer. They learn they can't be a dragon. They learn how to resent their lot in life. They learn how to not fit in their own skin. And we, too, were once children.

What would it be like to be a cat? I don't mean our stories about it. I don't mean imagining napping 20 hours a day, or being irresistibly drawn to chasing small moving objects, or clawing up the furniture because it feels good to crack our knuckles. I mean what would the actual experience be like, absent these narratives?

It's impossible to imagine, of course. We can't actually imagine being something completely different than what we are. But I think it's safe to say that cats can't think—certainly not in complex language the way humans can. So being a cat would be like... nothing. We're incapable of saying what it would be like, because if we were a cat we wouldn't be able to say what it was like. Or, here, another way to think about it: being a cat would be like what it was like when you were an infant. Do you recall that? Of course not. No one does, because we didn't have the mental tools to store complex memories. An infant appears to have an experience of being—as does a cat—but those experiences aren't the same thing as language.

And yet... somehow you and I and every other adult got from being that infant to being the adults we are today. What happened to the infants we used to be? Are they somehow metaphysically dead?

Or have we simply gotten so far out of practice with perceiving the world the way an infant does that we no longer remember how to do it?

I strongly suspect this latter interpretation. I think that we are, in fact, constantly perceiving the world in exactly the same way we did as infants—we just aren't aware that we're doing it because our heads are so full of thoughts and ideas and words and stories. I suspect that those narrative descriptions of reality are so psychically noisy that we forget they aren't real—that we confuse them with reality itself. Hence the dogma we discussed so thoroughly in the chapter on Big Idea #1. Hence our propensity to confuse our beliefs with reality.

But even though our beliefs are powerful—even though they can, as we mentioned, shape reality through the creation of social constructs—our beliefs are still subsidiary to actual reality. They are, at the end of the day, things we created. And so they are things we can uncreate.

For many people, the idea of uncreating their beliefs is terrifying. I can vaguely recall a time when that was the case for me. When imagining that I wouldn't go to heaven when I died started my heart racing, my palms sweating, anxiety surging in me like a storm. Well, look at that: a metaphor. A story. A narrative I was attached to. We don't seem to be able to escape them, do we?

No matter how much it may feel like our beliefs are true, no matter how much it may feel like our stories are reality, they are not.

To see why this is the case, we need to go into more detail about something I've mentioned previously, but haven't yet discussed: perspective.

When Renaissance painters were figuring out perspective, they realized something important: perspective had to do with lines. When we look at things in the real world, there is this optical phenomenon that parallel lines appear to converge toward a single point on the horizon. Here's a good example of pre-Renaissance art that seems to be unaware of this way of looking at things:

Used with permission from wga.hu

See how the shapes of the buildings are all different, how different people at the same distance from the viewer are different sizes, and how you can somehow see both sides of the same castle wall? It's as if the different objects in the painting were drawn at different times, from different perspectives. To our modern aesthetic eye, it just looks... lopsided.

———

Now, an example of a piece of art with Renaissance linear perspective:

Used with permission from wga.hu

In this painting, you can see how each row of columns falls along its own straight line, and that all those lines converge toward a single point in the background. This gives a much more realistic effect, as if we're viewing the scene from just a single perspective, and allows the people in the painting to be made larger or smaller in a way that makes it easy for our brain to locate them in the imaginary three-dimensional space of the painting.

But perspective is not just about a painting technique. It's related to how we must think about things. In the same way we discussed in Big Idea #1, perspective has to do with what things *look like* to us. It does not have to do with how things *are*. This, too, is a common mistake we tend to make. Like with the flat earth and round earth.

Or, again on the art theme: imagine you are standing in front of the Mona Lisa and I am standing behind it. You look at the painting and see a woman, while I am looking at a canvas and frame. Which of us is looking at the great art piece? Both of us are, of course. But which of us *can tell* we're looking at the great art piece?

What *looks* true to us is inevitably bound up in perspective. We can't escape that because whatever we are (which is what we're trying to discuss in this section of the book) appears to be tied to a perspective. We are looking out at a very large reality from a single point. This is the same as a cat, or an infant.

But what *is* true is... well, it's still unwordsable. Big Idea #1 still holds. But for the purposes of Big Idea #2, we need to ease up on truth a little bit. Looking at things from the perspective of Big Idea #1, I would say, for example, that the color red doesn't exist, that elephants don't exist, and that this book doesn't exist. From the perspective of all reality, these things are undifferentiated parts of the landscape.

But for the purposes of Big Idea #2, which moves from that undifferentiated whole to an individual perspective within it, whether or not we say something is true has entirely to do with what it looks like to us—and with our ability to honestly and effectively describe what it looks like. There's a tension here between these two levels of being. It can be difficult to simultaneously hold onto the idea that the table I'm sitting at is a real object from my little perspective, but at different places and times within the totality of reality it has been a seed, a tree, a pile of planks at the sawmill, or a scattering of cosmic dust—not to mention all the forms it will take as we continue to move forward into the future. Sometimes it seems like it would be better to be like the cat and just be unaware of this complexity and tension.

But, ironically, in order to be like the cat, we need to accept what we are. We need to let ourselves be human. And part of what it is to be human is to be stretched between these multiple perspectives. It makes sense for us to be aware of this, in the same way it makes sense for a cat to attack small moving things. Our ability to perceive things from multiple perspectives is unique within reality, and I think it's valuable—whether or not we can see or understand why.

The problem is that, most of the time, most of us are either unaware or forget about the dual nature of things.

If we were looking at the Mona Lisa from two sides and I stubbornly insisted I was looking only at a frame and a piece of canvas, I would be the idiot. And yet this is precisely what we do all day long. When we gather with our family or friends or on social media, we spin stories about the things that happened to us, or the things that happened to other people, or the things we think about other people, or the things the "other side" did. We do this constantly and nearly thoughtlessly, because such stories are a reflection of how we exist in the world: bound to a perspective.

Look at it this way: all day, every day, every time we hear a story or tell a story, we are *practicing* looking at things from a single perspective. We are *reinforcing* the idea that *what we perceive is what is* (which, as we've already discussed, isn't true). So it's no wonder we get confused and dismayed when we are confronted with the fact that what's true is much bigger and more complicated than our stories allow us to understand. We get dismayed when we encounter someone whose social constructs have taught them different lessons about the way the world works. We get dismayed when we find ourselves in a situation that our stories and the beliefs they're based on haven't equipped us to deal with.

So while our stories allow us to make sense of the world and move through it with a great deal of facility in most of the situations we encounter, they also limit us by preventing us from seeing other possible perspectives. They lock us into our own little worlds, which we then mistake for the real world. They enable our dogmas.

As an example of how stories limit us, I'll tell you a story. (Oh, the irony of being a human writing a book of words to try to explain how word-stories aren't real!)

There's a used bookstore in my town. I know the owner—let's call her Julie (not her real name)—through a friend. My friend was telling me that Julie was frustrated. She was frustrated by how busy she was all the time, keeping her small business open, running from location to location, hiring and firing employees, managing inventory and accounting. So much work, never a break. Caring all the time, trying all the time, and still having to put on a cheerful face for her customers. And all because of the business, right? Julie was trapped.

Of course, it's easy for you and me to see that's not true. Julie owns the business. She could choose to delegate if she wanted to. To reduce her work hours, hire someone to take on the responsibilities she was choosing to take on. Sure, those kinds of changes come with logistical challenges, but the problems aren't unsolvable. There must be lots of small-business owners out there—even bookstore owners—who don't feel constantly put-upon by the very existence of their business. And even if the problems aren't unsolvable, it's Julie's business. She can choose to close her doors at any time.

Julie wasn't trapped by her business. She was trapped by the perspective-based story she had been telling herself for years—a story in which she played an important role. The mistake is that she forgot she was playing a role. You and I can easily see what had Julie trapped. It wasn't her business. It was the fact that she confused the role with *who she was.* And so the cause of all her unhappiness, frustration, and overwhelm was actually herself the entire time. She just forgot how to recognize that she was not the role: the businessperson, entrepreneur, boss, successful self-made woman. Julie was trapped because of Julie, and no one else.

We can learn from Julie's situation that so often when we get tied up in knots, stressed out, angry, hopeless, frustrated, depressed, or fed up, one of the biggest reasons—if not the biggest reason—is that we've forgotten we agreed to play a role within whatever social constructs make up our world at that point in time. In other words, that we are complicit in our lives being the way they are. And, like Julie, we continue to beat our heads against whatever walls we've constructed for ourselves, failing to realize we created them purely out of belief. Belief and storytelling, both based in perspective.

So what's the way out of this trap? I've hinted at it already. We started Big Idea #2 talking about it. I took us on this detour through perspective and story to try to help you see them for what they are, but the answer—the key to this lock on our trap —is recognizing *what you are*. Not who you are; *what* you are. There is an important distinction.

What you are is almost exactly the same as the exercise I suggested to you earlier, when I had you try to imagine you were a cat. It's not that you can't imagine what it's like to be a cat— it's that you can't *describe* it. As soon as you try to tell a story about it, you've placed a human narrative perspective onto the experience. And being a cat would only be like... a very cattish experience. No cat ever resents being a cat, or gets trapped in perspective-based socially constructed stories about itself.

Well, the same is true of human infants. They don't ever resent being human. It is only we adults who get all tied up in knots about our lives.

You see where I'm going here, right? You were once an infant. So you used to know how to not be trapped in this way. You just forgot. You learned how to tell stories, then you learned how to tell stories from your own perspective, then you learned how to play the roles in the stories you were telling, then you learned how to forget that you were telling a story in the first place.

So the way out of the trap is to remember. To remember what it's like to be a human being. But no, that's not so helpful because all of us have so many stories attached to the term human being. Maybe it's better to say we need to remember what it's like to be an infant. We all have our infant selves inside us, somewhere. Or maybe it's even better to just say we need to remember what it's like just to *be*. Just *being*. To set all the stories and the words down for a moment and just notice, just be aware of reality happening around you and within you. We could try to imagine what it's like to be a cat, but why not try instead to just experience what it's like to be a human? To be a human, except with the stories turned off for a while. To silence the narrative in our heads. To just look at the forest in silence, and feel that we're a part of it. I can do the same thing here in my dining room, early in the morning. I just... forget... most of the time. And remembering is a habit I need to work on.

What I'm talking about here is actually what I think people set out to practice when they do meditation. Thinking—storytelling—is a tool, and meditation is practice at setting that tool down, at stopping the incessant flow of thoughts and just looking out at the world as would a cat or an infant. With a perspective, yes, and a set of senses for perceiving. Yet with none of the judgments or attachments that we normally connect to that perception, unaware of how it is coloring, even distorting, what we perceive.

All great progress in human history has come when people have *noticed* something. The linear perspective of Renaissance paintings was always there. But painters before the Renaissance didn't notice it. They just continued doing things the way they had always done them. But someone, somewhen, or a group of someones, were able to set down the way they had learned to look at the world, and *notice* how lines seem to converge on a single point in the distance in a human perspective of reality.

What as-yet unnoticed things do you think might be out

there right now, just waiting for the right person to quiet their mind and sit in silent observation of reality? What things do you think you might notice if you were to do this?

"The taste of coffee lingers on my tongue. I take a slow, deep breath through my nose, savoring the feeling of it filling my lungs. I am slouched and relaxed in my chair. I send a quick prayer to whatever it is that's listening (if anything is), asking for help with today's writing, and in a larger way with the whole book. I feel confident that I will produce something that will help someone."

I wrote that paragraph months ago. I don't even remember when. I just copied and pasted it in here because it was the beginning of this same section of the book in an earlier draft. Today, I can say in all honesty that I'm full of doubt that this book will help anyone. I'm struggling with what order to include the ideas, with how to articulate them, and with imagining who you, my reader, are, and how my words might help you.

How can the same person—me—feel such different, contradictory feelings? Well, I don't know. But I can think of one thing that's the same between the person who wrote the first paragraph and the person who wrote the second: the *fact* of his existence (as contrasted with the *contents*—or the narrative—of his existence).

We get so caught up in our thoughts, our stories about what's happening to us at any given time. But it's possible to set those thoughts and stories aside and just pay Attention. I'll try to describe what that's like.

Right now, in this moment, I see the glow of my computer screen in the darkness of my dining room. It lights my hands, fingers curled over the keys as they tap-tap-tap away, sometimes in short bursts as I struggle to find a particular word, sometimes in the extended forays of a more fully formed idea. During a particularly long pause, I glance to my right and gaze at the salt lamp for a few moments, my mind hazy in the early morning. I take another sip of coffee, and type this sentence. And then this one. I notice again my hands, connected to my shadowed wrists, pointing down and outward toward the edges of my vision. My arms disappear into the yet deeper darkness of my bathrobe, eventually passing out of my field of view. Right at the edges of what I can see while continuing to watch these words appear, I see my shoulder-length hair framing the scene, moving a bit, from time to time, as I tilt my head or give a twitch. I decide to stop writing after this sentence so I can go to the bathroom.

Well, that was mostly boring and private. It's a good thing other people usually can't see what our lives look like from our perspectives. It would make for incredibly dull television.

But, joking aside, what I want to point out to you is the thing I just described, but about *yourself*. What are you doing right now? There you sit, reading this paragraph. Perhaps you're on the couch or a comfy chair, feet propped before you. Perhaps you're on the bus or train, surrounded by other people with no idea of the story unfolding in your experience just a few feet away from them. Stop reading and take a moment to just watch what this moment in your life looks like. Don't think about it, don't narrate it, don't get attached to it. Just watch. Go ahead, give it a try.

What I'm trying to help you notice in this book is your own experience of being. Not your experience of thinking; thinking is subsidiary to being. Thinking *proceeds* from being. (Yes, I think Descartes was wrong.) No, I just mean your experience of being.

In theater, we use the phrase "breaking the fourth wall" to refer to the situation when a character speaks directly to the audience, as if they are aware of the audience's existence and their own existence as just a character in a show. Marvel's *Deadpool* is famous for using this literary device.

What I want to show you is how to break your *own* fourth wall. To see the way in which your life is a show. You can participate in it, as we all do day in and day out. But, from time to time, you can also take a break and just watch. Both are simply tools for engaging with reality. Neither is better or worse. They are just responses we can choose. The Western world of the Enlightenment is, for the most part, in the habit of always choosing to participate in the show. That is where productivity lies, where self-interest lies. That is where problems get solved and progress gets made. The enlightened Eastern world more often chooses to let things be what they are, and just watch. It sees the connections between things and accepts the world as it is. This way of looking at things is not better or worse than the way of the Enlightenment. It's simply a different, and equally valuable, tool. A different, and equally valuable, perspective.

Here, I'll walk you through an exercise in two stages.

Imagine you are in a movie theater. The movie is already playing on the screen. But this movie is a little different. Rather than just seeing and hearing the movie, you can also smell what you see on the screen. If it's a forest, you can smell the trees. If it's raining, you can smell the petrichor. And it's not just smell— no, you can feel the movie, too: the wind across your face, or the rumble of a waterfall nearby. In fact, now that you think about it, you can sense the movie in every way. You find your point of view anchored to the camera. You don't really have any agency, you're just along for the ride. But the sensory experience is completely engrossing. It feels entirely as if you are there, right in the movie. But at the same time, you are aware that you are just watching a movie, and that somewhere back in the theater is your body, safe and comfortable in its seat.

Now, let's shift this a bit. Instead of being in a movie theater, come back to the present moment. You are reading this book. Perhaps you're at home, sitting on the sofa, book in hand. But, rather than being the one holding the book, reading the book, imagine that, just like in the movie theater, you are only watching this happen. You are only observing events. You are not sitting on the sofa; *someone* is sitting on a sofa. You are not reading a book; *someone* is reading a book. Try to imagine, same as if you were in that movie theater, but now you have two added senses: interoception (meaning you sense a body), and cognition (meaning you can 'hear' thoughts in your mind). For now, though, try to hold onto the idea that you are only observing those two senses. You are just watching a movie: the movie about what's happening to you right now.

The person looks around the room, noticing several details, then looks back at the book and reads the next paragraph.

The person takes a deep breath, feeling the air flow into, then out of, their chest and belly.

The person feels the couch or chair they're sitting on. They notice where they're comfortable, and where they're uncomfortable—but they understand they don't need to make any adjustments. Any discomfort is acceptable, for the moment. All they need to do is notice.

The person pauses for a moment, closes their eyes, and listens to their thoughts. They notice the same things again: where the thoughts are comfortable, and where they're uncomfortable. Again they understand they don't need to make any adjustments. Any discomfort is acceptable, for the moment. All they need to do is notice.

After a moment has passed, they return to the book and read this sentence.

So. Did you catch a glimpse of it? This moment isn't something you're *doing*. It's simply happening. And you are the one *watching* it happen. There are things in this moment: the details you noticed about the room, the breath you felt, the couch or chair you're sitting on—*and the thoughts you're hearing*. The thoughts aren't *you*. They are just another thing your body is doing—the same as breathing and feeling the breath, the same as sitting and feeling whatever you're sitting on. Thoughts are just another thing happening in this moment—another thing you're watching happen.

*You* are the one watching this movie. It is, in a way, exactly like being in a theater, but instead of just watching the movie with your eyes, you're watching it with your whole awareness. And, just like you can't see your own eyes with your eyes, you can't see your own awareness with your awareness.

There are a few words people use to describe this core awareness: soul, spirit, seat of consciousness, core self. It's important to maintain the distinction between the words we use to describe things and the things themselves. The experience of being present can only be perfectly described in zero words. I can say "my soul," but what I mean is not some thing that can be abstracted into a simple four-letter word like that. What I mean is this all-encompassing awareness of *being*, right here, right now, in this moment.

We can try to talk about it, but really we can only experience it. What I'm trying to point to is the same thing as being a cat, because your awareness of a human being is the same as the awareness of a cat. You have a human body and mind, yes, and a cat has a cat body and mind. But you also have an awareness of your body and mind, just like a cat has an awareness of its body and mind. It's only the content and complexity of your thoughts that are different. The thing that makes us different from the other animals is not inherent to our *existence*; it's inherent to our *thinking*. The way we are aware that we are aware—that we are not just conscious, but *self-conscious*—is only possible when we use the mental technology of language. When we set language down, even for a little while, we get what seems to be a deeper, truer experience of this present moment.

This sort of unwordsable just-being, here in the present moment, is about as close to bedrock as we can get with experience. There is a question here, teetering on a knife's edge: is your awareness something your mind is doing, or is your mind something your awareness is aware of? (4.1)

I used to believe it was the first one—that my awareness was something my mind was doing. But, more and more, as I have gained experience, I think it's the second. My mind is something my awareness is aware of.

---

4.1 At this level, it can be really difficult to distinguish between thought and belief. Indeed, in the next few paragraphs you will see me use the words almost interchangeably. Despite that we might like to think otherwise, there is some recent psychological and sociological research that suggests the vast majority of the time our thoughts proceed from our beliefs without influencing them at all. In other words, something like 90% of the time our thoughts are justifications attempting to defend our beliefs, rather than actual reasons for why we believe what we do. I know that we all think we're immune to this, but the truth seems to be that we believe what we believe, based on our experience and our perspective, and that our thinking is a follow-on effect of those beliefs. This relationship between our thoughts and beliefs is, of course, a big part of the problem we're looking at in this book. There isn't necessarily anything wrong with belief preceding thought. But it does carry the risk of harmful dogma, and therefore suffering. What I am arguing in this section is that we should try to learn to better differentiate our thinking from our beliefs so that we can make better decisions about what we think and believe. And if we are capable of changing our beliefs 10% of the time, we can learn to do it more often. In fact, I think we have a responsibility—a response-ability—to learn to do it more often. In the following paragraphs, I did my best to pay close Attention to whether my beliefs were influencing my thoughts, or my thoughts were trying to inform my beliefs.

I'll tell you what I believe are my reasons for thinking this, but even if they don't change your mind about what you believe, I hope you will have gained valuable insight into what seem to me to be two mutually exclusive ways of looking at what's going on inside your experience of being. Even if we have a difference of opinion—or perspective, depending on how you look at it—we should be able to proceed with a precise understanding of our disagreement, and the fact that it is about the smallest imaginable disagreement.

The real reason I believe my awareness precedes my mind is because when I pay Attention, that seems to be how I experience things. Now, I'm contradicting myself a bit, because earlier I said that believing something to be true because it looks like it's true isn't a very good reason to believe something. (4.2)

I admit to this contradiction in an attempt to be transparent that this is just a belief. And our little beliefs, based on our limited little perspectives, will inevitably seem contradictory in some way when they bump up against the vastness of reality. That is not, of course, a good reason to cling to them when a better belief presents itself. But, to me, this seems like the best description of my experience I have found. I present it to you here in the hopes that it will help you pay better Attention to your own experience of being, and decide for yourself what you think is true. So, with that admission, let's proceed.

---

4.2 I also said we're in the unfortunate position of "because it looks like it" being the best we can do sometimes. Normally we mitigate our faulty perception by using multiple tools to verify something. That's why we have five senses, for example. Something you can only see is less likely to be real than something you can see, hear, smell, taste, and feel. But when it comes to my inner existence, the only tool I have to verify it is my own experience of it.

———

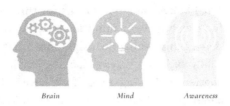

Because I'm describing a model, we're about to go pretty far down in the weeds. Keep in mind that a model is a kind of definition, and definitions are always trying to point to real things in reality. This model is trying to describe your own experience— so remember to check in with your own experience throughout this section. Hopefully that will help you see both the forest and the tree here.

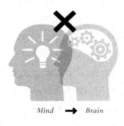

*Diagram 1*

I consider a mind to be something like a collection of thoughts—perhaps even, given a particular person's lived experiences, a collection of *possible* thoughts. Now, I think everyone would agree that their mind is something created by their brain. Our thoughts happen "in" our brains. Or, more precisely, thoughts are something brains do. It's not the other way around: our brains don't exist because of our thoughts.

Look at it this way: if modern science and medicine hadn't taught us that we use our brains to think, the only thing we would be aware of is thinking. We wouldn't be aware of our brains at all. So the brain must precede thought. Therefore the brain precedes mind.

Having eliminated this potential starting point, I see four possibilities, which I've represented in the diagrams below.

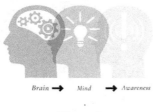

Brain ➡  Mind  ➡ Awareness

*Diagram 2*

Diagram 2 describes Descartes' idea, "I think, therefore I am." I think it's a bad model because when I look at infants, they seem to have an experience of existing, but they don't seem to be able to think. For example, a baby knows when it's hungry, as evidenced by its cries for food, but I doubt it is thinking anything like, "I am hungry." Thinking—at least insofar as we are familiar with it—requires language. I would argue that we learn to think as we learn language.

Now, I used to be an infant, which means I used to be unable to think. If this model is accurate, that would mean I didn't exist when I was an infant. But that seems absurd, so the model must be inaccurate.

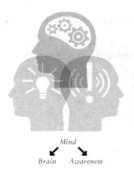

*Diagram 3*

Diagram 3 describes a situation where awareness and mind are separate things which both arise in the brain. It's a neat solution to the objection I raise above. If it's a good model, then infant Michael *could* have had an awareness, proceeding from his brain, and could still have spent the next few decades constructing his mind, the evidence of which you are reading at this moment.

However, I still think it falls short. Look at any plant as an example of why—I have one here, in front of me, on the table, next to the window. I haven't always thought of plants as having awareness, but after some close observation and contemplation, it seems inevitable to me that they must. They "know" what direction the sunlight is coming from, and how to grow toward it. They "know" where the soil is, and push roots down into it; in other words, they grow toward soil differently than they grow toward light.

But plants don't have brains, certainly—at least not organic brains like we humans have. To me, the conclusion seems to be that awareness isn't dependent upon a brain, so the model must be inaccurate.

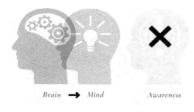

*Brain* → *Mind*        *Awareness*

*Diagram 4*

Diagram 4 shows a situation where the mind exists in the brain, and awareness is just an illusion. It doesn't really exist. It is somewhat the opposite of what I am trying to argue in this section: that our awareness is real and our mind a kind of illusion.

I readily admit this is a model I see no effective argument against. If awareness is an illusion created by our minds, then any argument I make to you about why it seems wrong would simply be me, an imaginary automaton, arguing with you, another imaginary automaton. Perhaps the best thing I can say is this: if this model is true, then "self" is not real. The only response I can see to the idea that I'm not real is nihilism. Meaninglessness, purposelessness. And, as I discussed previously, nihilism is a short, dark path to nonexistence—not just for you or me, but for all humanity. Human beings seem to need a reason to live. And I believe I have one.

So ultimately, I think this model is wrong because it *feels* wrong. I think the human will to live and love and create stands in direct opposition to the idea that existence is meaningless because awareness is an illusion. If that's not a good enough argument for you, then you are a very strong skeptic indeed, and we may simply end up disagreeing. But I still hope the rest of Big Idea #2 and Big Idea #3 will point out some things you haven't yet considered.

Awareness ➔ Brain ➔ Mind

*Diagram 5*

Our final diagram shows what I am trying to describe: ineffable awareness preceding brain, brain creating mind. I don't really know what awareness *is*. Perhaps it's some kind of force, some fundamental expression of reality. Maybe the reason matter doesn't pass through other matter is because it somehow "knows" it isn't "supposed" to.

I won't pretend to know. All I will say is that this model *seems* to be the way I exist. It is what my existence "looks like" to my conscious self, and my conscious self is, as far as I can tell, the only witness to my mental/spiritual existence. There's no one else "in here" with me.

It's time to pull ourselves up from being down in these weeds. Let's come up with some terms to make it a little easier to talk about these things.

The real trouble here is distinguishing between these two different parts of ourselves: what I've been calling mind and awareness. What I'm calling mind is the part of us we use to think thoughts, so let's use the term *thinker* to refer to mind.

The problem I'm trying to point out in Big Idea #2 is the fact that we get confused by our thinker. We often fall under the illusion that we *are* our thinker. But I don't believe that's true. My thinker isn't *me*. I believe this because *I am in control of my thinker*, and not the other way around.

Here, look:

I am not a hand. I know this because I am in control of my hand. I can relax it, set it down, and let it lie there, subject to gravity and inertia and friction and convection and all the other physical forces that influence it but which I am not in control of.

*In exactly the same way*, I am not a mind. I know this because I am in control of my mind. I can relax it, set it down, stop it from bombarding me with a barrage of words, and let it, too, be subject in its own way to the physical forces of the universe.

I don't *have to* think, anymore than I *have to* use my hands. Cut off my hands, and *I* still exist. Remove my mind, either through madness, dementia, or rewinding time back to when I was an infant, and *I* still exist.

So if I am not a hand, and I am not a mind, then I am not any of the other parts of myself I can manipulate. So what's left? Who is this person controlling this thinker that's writing this book to you?

Well, what's the only thing left? I must be the thing that's aware of the hand and the mind and all the other parts. That thing is my conscious awareness of being—what I call, to contrast it with my thinker, my *Observer*. I am, as the subtitle of this chapter says, *that which perceives*. And so, I think *and* believe, are you.

I can "turn off" my thoughts. I can't turn off my awareness. Yes, I go to sleep every night, but there's still some low-level awareness going on there, tracking the passage of time, for example, or observing my dreams. I know when I've been asleep because I was aware of being asleep.

My Observer is me. I am my Observer. I think the fact that I can distinguish between them in sentences like those is a side effect of language; in order to try to communicate this idea to you, I need a word to refer to it. But there isn't a word for it. There is no way to communicate it. It's unwordsable—like what being a cat would be like. My Observer doesn't understand language. Maybe it knows that my thinker understands language. It gets hard to say.

The thing about thinking of myself this way is that it gives me a consistent thread of "me-ness" that I can trace back all the way to the beginning of my life and trace forward all the way to the end. My awareness is the same today as it was yesterday, and the day before, and the day before. It never changes. Sure, each day is filled up with different experiences and feelings and memories, but the pure fact of my awareness has always been exactly the same. Now that I realize this, it seems absurd that it's taken me so long to understand that tomorrow I will be the same as I will be the day after that, as I will be any random day in five or ten or fifty years. My Observer doesn't change. So I don't change. It's only the circumstances that surround me that change.

Part of those circumstances are my identity.

Now, this may be a little challenging. We don't usually think about identity this way, because it can be uncomfortable. So I'll go ahead and tell you the story from my own perspective. It's a lot like the example from earlier, when Julie was thinking of herself as a bookstore owner. Except in this case, the story is much more pervasive.

My whole life, my thinker has been told this story, and my Observer has watched that process. The story I've been told is that I am Michael Marvosh. The story of Michael Marvosh was originally dreamed up by my parents. Well, the Michael part of it was. The Marvosh part was dreamed up long ago by someone of Slavic descent, somewhere in what today we call Eastern Europe.

As my thinker learned more and more about that story, it began to tell it itself. It selected things it thought I should be interested in, and things it thought I should be less interested in. It selected clothes it thought I liked and disliked, music it thought I was drawn to, activities it thought I wanted to pursue and other activities that were too boring or difficult, or which I just happened to have a sufficiently bad day with. My thinker did this to be helpful, because in a functionally unlimited reality, survival requires finding things we enjoy, because those are the things that are most likely to keep us alive. So, Michael Marvosh likes cherries more than oranges, baseball more than soccer, singing better than playing the guitar, board games better than puzzles, riddles better than pranks. He likes truth better than stories (but he realizes the power and importance of stories).

"I am Michael Marvosh." That's a story. That's a role I'm playing. Michael Marvosh is just a story—he doesn't exist, not really. He's just a reference, like "red," or "elephant," or "business owner," a narrative tool you and I can use to talk about a specific entity who *does* exist (the body in which resides my Observer—the one currently watching these words appear on Michael's computer screen).

So why do I continue to maintain the illusory notion of Michael Marvosh? I do it in part because I'm used to it, and in part, because like so many of our stories, it's useful. It's useful for me for interacting with other people, for them to interact with me, to have relationships, to get married, have children, write and publish a book, to get paid for my work. If the idea of Michael Marvosh didn't exist, I wouldn't be able to receive mail or own a home, to have beliefs or hopes and dreams for myself and my life. Without Michael Marvosh I wouldn't be a human being.

It gives me no anxiety to admit this. I'm not saying *I* don't exist. I can say with more confidence than anything that *I* exist: I am the one watching this sentence appear on a computer screen.

No, what I am saying is that *Michael Marvosh* doesn't exist. Michael Marvosh is just a social construct. Michael Marvosh is my identity, given to me in part by my family, in part by my society and culture, in part by my physiology and experiences, in part by my will. Michael Marvosh changes every day—changes, in fact, with each moment of experience I have. But I, the conscious awareness behind Michael Marvosh's eyes that I call Observer, never change. I am the same today as I was when he was born—even though I can't remember it. I am the same today as I was yesterday, the same as I will be tomorrow, the same as I will be when I close his eyes for the last time and pass from this existence.

And I say this with the utmost gentleness and compassion: the same is true of you.

It took me a lot of practice, but now when I do exercises like we discussed earlier, where I just watch what's going on while trying to avoid telling stories about it—trying to avoid any kind of narrative at all—I notice this kind of quiet, soft sufficiency. I feel myself breathing, and each breath is like an intimate conjoining with the air—with reality's air. I rub the tips of my fingers together and feel the tenderness of a moment where nothing is demanded of me, nothing expected. I don't have to justify or explain or perform. All I need to do is be, and notice that I am. What could be easier than that?

I also become aware that this quiet moment to myself, within myself, is not fundamentally different than the moments of my life full of chaos and noise, or conflict and anxiety. I could also, in those moments, if I were good enough at it, choose to simply set aside my narratives about what's going on and just watch. Just be.

It's certainly more difficult when there's a lot of distracting stuff happening. But the reality of this moment and the reality of more chaotic moments are the same reality. One is, perhaps, the forest, the other the tree. As we've already discussed.

But, now that we've descended to the deepest part of our being and took note of what was there, we need to turn back. We need to consider the effects of looking at ourselves and each other this way.

Before we do, please know that you can come back to this "place" at any time. Your Observer is always with you, always ready for a quiet moment. And, though we'll talk about this more in Big Idea #3, your Observer always loves you. If ever you find yourself suffering some negative self-talk, try to remember that it is your thinker doing the talking. And your thinker just learned to talk that way by imitating the people around it. It's not your Observer. It's not you. You can set down your thoughts for a moment, whenever you want.

But, I mentioned suffering, and, unfortunately, suffering is the thing we'll take special notice of on our path back up from here. Recall our definition of suffering from earlier. Suffering is pain plus resistance. Suffering is when we are squirming in discomfort, trying to deny the reality of what's happening right now, in this present moment.

Notice how, when you are simply watching this present moment passing, there is no room for suffering. What is happening is simply happening. What is, is. You are just a bystander, a witness, and there is nothing wrong with your next breath, or the feeling of your fingertips against these pages, or the opinions of that random person over there—or, for that matter, your own opinions. All those things are just things that exist, in this moment. They become stressful and scary and threatening—in other words, they cause us to suffer—when we judge them. But nothing says we need to be constantly judging the world around us. Nothing, that is, except the thinking brain we learned to use as children.

Even when your body is in pain, when it has an injury or illness, you are not your body. The pain is just another thing that is happening, that you are watching. Even when your thoughts are in turmoil, trying to bite themselves, to lash out in habitual cruelty or negativity or judgment, you can just watch that, too. Just notice it. And, maybe, with a little practice, you can start letting those thoughts go. The more you do, the more you will be able to see that all your suffering is actually inflicted on you by your thinker—and that when it inflicts suffering on you, you also inadvertently inflict it on those around you. On everyone, in fact. But, sadly, especially on those you love.

This is difficult stuff to talk about. I mean that in a couple different ways.

For one thing, it's difficult to articulate. It's not obvious. I've written and rewritten again and again in the hopes that I can make it clear, and I still fear I have failed.

But for another thing, it's hard for your thinker to hear that it's not real. Your thinker doesn't want to be not real. Why do you think the story of Pinocchio has stuck with us for so long? It's because it captures the conflict between our thinker's desire to become real and our Observer's knowing, on some level, that it's all a lie, its nose ever growing.

We've already considered the term for when someone achieves total recognition of the reality of their Observer and the unreality of their thinker: it's called enlightenment. Enlightenment is what allows Buddhist monks to burn themselves to death in protest of great injustice. Not that I'm suggesting that's what any of us should do, or even be able to do. I think we all need to try to get along. I just also think that we should try to recognize the truth of what we are.

There is, during the time I am writing this book, a growing mindfulness movement. I don't know that I would say it's being led by any individual person—or even that any individual person would want to do something like lead a mindfulness movement. But when I hear some of the most well-known voices of the movement speak—voices like that of Eckhart Tolle, for instance—it seems to me that they are getting things ever-so-slightly backwards.

It seems to me that the mindfulness movement is saying that the Observer is more important than the thinker, and that we should try to be like those Buddhist monks: try to fix ourselves in the seat of the Observer, and to watch the thinker going about its oh-so human business 100% of the time.

I think there is something to be said for this. It's an under-standable response, especially to extreme levels of suffering. When the thinker is the source of suffering, a desire for the suffering to end can lead one to retreat from the thinker altogether.

But to deny the existence of the thinker seems to go too far, to me. Each of us created our thinkers to help us survive. When we were babies, and all we had was an Observer, we were help-less. The other people in our lives taught us to construct a thinker, and that thinker helped each of us get to where we are —and more than that, it helped all of humanity to get to where it is. For better or worse, the thinker has installed itself as a vital facet of human existence. It's made itself a necessary tool for us —the same as evolution made our opposable thumbs a neces-sary tool for us.

If suffering entered the world because the thinker forgot about the Observer's existence, then will not a similar amount of suffering enter the world if the Observer forgets about the thinker? In other words, we shouldn't amputate our thinkers any more than we should amputate our thumbs.

I think what we need to find, as it is with so many things, is balance. The Observer and the thinker can also be looked at as different tools. And we should always try to use the right tool for the job. When we need to understand something, we need to perceive it as accurately as possible. That's what the Observer is good at. The thinker makes mistakes when it comes to perceiving because it thinks it already understands things. But, of course, things are more complicated than it can imagine. As discussed in Big Idea #1, things are *infinitely* complicated. On the other hand, when we need to solve a problem, that requires thinking—and the Observer isn't the right tool for thinking. The thinker's job is to solve the specific problems of survival. That's a valuable job, and we should work to keep the tool we use to do it —the thinker—sharp.

For the last several hundred thousand years the survival of humanity has required the work of the thinker. As we have spread across the planet, we have solved problem after problem. And yet now we are bumping up against a problem our collective thinker seems unable to solve, because it doesn't understand it. The thinker only understands things from the perspective of keeping the physical organism alive. It has forgotten about the Observer riding along with each of us, watching reality unfold into the future.

The thinker has been working incredibly hard at nurturing human survival. But now we are beginning to discover its limits.

We are seeing that too much human survival is itself bad for human survival. And that's a conundrum the thinker is not equipped to solve. It's the wrong tool for the job.

I think the future of humanity, if it is to continue, is going to require one of two things: either we need a spiritual reawakening to the fact of our Observers, so that we can use the right tool for the job at hand, or we need to, through technology, create a new tool. And, actually, I don't think these two solutions are mutually exclusive. In fact, I think a technological solution might be the only very-long-term solution. But if the creation of that technology is informed only by our thinkers, then it will be based on a too-limited understanding of reality.

Whether or not humanity's path into the future is one of spiritual awakening or technological innovation, one thing seems clear to me: we need to give the Observer a seat at the table again.

## CHAPTER FIVE
# BIG IDEA #3

*To live in this world*

*you must be able*
*to do three things:*
*to love what is mortal;*
*to hold it*

*against your bones knowing*
*your own life depends on it;*
*and, when the time comes to let it go,*
*to let it go.*

*— MARY OLIVER, "IN BLACKWATER*
*WOODS," EXCERPT*

## INTRODUCTION

WHAT ARE WE TO DO WHEN WE REALIZE THAT OUR PERSPECTIVE-BASED names for things confuse us just as easily as they empower us? We can experience—and notice the difference between—

running into a tree and running into a forest. One hurts, while the other is simply a nice afternoon activity. But this difference only exists because of how big we happen to be. Trees are roughly us-sized, while forests are big enough that we can easily slip between the things that make them up.

Were we smaller, like a beetle or a microbe, trees would be like forests to us. We could perceive their nooks and crannies and passageways and move through them as easily as a human might move through a forest. And the forest, well... to us microscopic things, something as big as a forest would be beyond imagining.

So you see that forest and tree, while not entirely arbitrary terms, are at least an amount of arbitrary relative to our size and position within reality. All things are made up of smaller things, and all small things can be thought of as part of something bigger. It is our thinker that chops things up into pieces and figures out how to use the pieces to survive. Our Observer is just along for the ride.

Sometimes I imagine what the Observers of people who came before me must have witnessed, and I find myself flabbergasted. What must it have been like to uproot your family and all your possessions in the American East, and load it all into a covered wagon for a months long trip on the Oregon Trail, across thousands of miles of wilderness?

What must it have been like for the first humans who crossed the land bridge from Asia to have looked down on the wild land they had discovered and find it crawling with monsters? I mean literal monsters, like saber-toothed tigers, giant ground sloths, woolly mammoths, cave bears, dire wolves, and vultures with 12-foot wingspans. I would have immediately turned around and gone back the way I came, but I imagine them giving a terse grunt, rolling up their sleeves, and getting to work figuring out how to hunt all these giants to extinction.

Of course, it's a little self-indulgent to dream about the

Observed experiences of those who have gone before, when there is plenty of mind-boggling suffering going on today. People are boarding boats in the Gulf of Mexico to try to emigrate to the United States, not knowing if they'll make it or die in the attempt. People are fleeing war-torn countries with little more than the clothes on their backs, and if they manage to escape with their lives they have the daunting task not only of finding a country that will accept them, but also of figuring out how to make a living in a new place, not knowing the language or the customs. It's difficult to imagine. And I often wonder what more I could be doing to try to help alleviate that suffering. Is writing a book like this the right thing to do? What a troubling privilege...

And yet, this feels like what it's been given to me to do, given my *own* Observed experience. If there is something wrong with the world, or something missing from it, then the only place I can look for it is within myself. Tolstoy said, "Everyone thinks of changing the world, but no one thinks of changing himself." He's identified a great irony, hasn't he? That we all look out at the forest of the world and judge what's wrong about it, and what we think ought to change, while blithely overlooking the fact that we are the trees that make up the world, and that if we are to have any control at all, it must be first and foremost over ourselves.

But that is not cause for despair, or overwhelm. It is not a reason to give up. Because if the forest is the tree, then the tree is also the forest. And if we change ourselves, then we do change the world—even if only in a small way. The good news is that we are small, and mostly ignorant, and we can't predict what effect our changes will have. If you want to change the world, the only sensible choice is to start with changing yourself.

Why don't more people understand this? I think it's partly because we're distracted by our thinker's narrative, but it goes deeper than that. The narrative exists for a reason, and I think that reason is often to distract us from the truth, which is that we are afraid. Afraid to try. Afraid we will fail. Afraid we will experience pain. Afraid our efforts will be insufficient and ultimately meaningless. Afraid, ultimately, that we will die.

All these fears are certainly understandable. I recognize them in myself every day—even in the process of writing this book, which is a pretty safe undertaking when compared to all the other things people have gone and are going through. I don't think how safe something is has much to do with how afraid we are of it. No, what we need to rediscover is something that helps us recognize our fear and take action in spite of it.

The next chapter of the book—Big Idea #3—is about that thing.

———

## BIG IDEA #3: LOVE IS REAL, AND YOU ARE LOVED

There are two things we need to establish at the beginning of this section in order to talk about why and how you are loved.

The first is that emotions are not what you think they are.

The second is that, even if emotions *were* what you think they are, love is not an emotion.

I'm going to show you these two things because I suspect most people never learned how to notice love—at least not in the way that I'll be talking about it in this section (and, I suspect, for the rest of my life). Now, don't get me wrong: people know whether or not they're *in* love. Being in love definitely feels emotional. But, well. I'm getting ahead of myself. First, we need to look at what emotions are.

Emotions are pretty straightforward, right? We all have them; they're inner states that our body and/or mind take in response to different stimuli. For example, when something good happens, we feel happy, which energizes us to connect with others and seek more of that kind of experience. When something bad happens, we feel angry or disappointed, which causes us to withdraw from that experience and try to avoid it in the future. Happy and angry are emotions that prompt us to follow our pleasure/pain responses. All the other more nuanced emotions are simply more of the same. Sadness is a prompt that hopes to elicit support from those around us. Disgust is a prompt that hopes to keep us away from things that seem likely to make us sick. And love is a prompt that makes us want to care for someone or something. Right? That's the familiar idea of emotions? (5.1)

There is some interesting research that suggests this way of looking at emotions isn't quite correct. Let's look at two examples.

The first example has to do with how we perceive things.

Within the recent past it's become possible, through modern medicine and surgery, to give people who were born blind the ability to see, either by repairing their eyes or implanting functional ones. One unexpected thing that's been observed is that adults who have only just gained the ability to see can't actually perceive very much. For instance, if I were to put an apple in front of you, you would be able to see it and say it was an apple. But if you put an apple in front of an adult who has only just gained the ability to see for the first time, all they could see was... *something*. A smudge, or a light/dark spot (light and dark are the first things these people are able to perceive). Only when they experience the apple with their other senses, and actively pay an inordinate amount of Attention to their new visual cues, and are

---

5.1 Note that the wide range of situations in which we use the word love makes it challenging to talk about. We talk about love in regards to sex, to partnership, to parenting, to friendship, even to foods or activities we particularly enjoy. In using the words "care for," I am trying to find a way of encapsulating all those things. Because if we use the same word to refer to all of them, then they all must at least seem to have something in common—even if we aren't clear on what that thing is.

told the object is an apple, do they begin to be able to differentiate it. In other words, prior to *learning how to notice an apple*, these patients can't distinguish it from the rest of the visual background noise. What this suggests is that, as infants, each of us had to *learn how to see*.

Though this may initially seem a little unintuitive, when you give it some more thought it definitely makes sense. We've already discussed how a newborn human is a lot more like a cat than like an adult person. We need to teach babies that they have—as the song says—a "head, shoulders, knees, and toes." We need to teach them that they have one, two, three, four, five fingers. Their brains don't know these things inherently. They aren't born with a thinker; they have to construct one. Why should it be any different with vision? It doesn't make much sense to think that some of our perceptions are constructed in our mind while others are not. No, the more science shows us about how we perceive, the more it seems that *all* our perceptions are constructed. This idea aligns closely with Big Idea #1, suggesting that how we perceive reality is necessarily very different from how reality actually is. And that we therefore can't really talk about reality, but only about our perspective-bound perceptions of it.

And if all our perceptions are constructed, then the same must be true of our emotions. Including, yes, love. (Though love is not an emotion, it's a lot like one.)

The second of our two examples directly reinforces the idea that emotions are mental constructs that we learned to build, rather than feelings somehow inherent to our being.

In the 1960s, a team of anthropologists, Renato and Michelle Rosaldo (who were married to one another), embedded themselves with the Ilongot, a tribe of indigenous peoples in the Philippines. The Ilongot are headhunters; they will occasionally hunt down a person from another tribe, kill them, and decapitate them. This is somewhat distasteful to us, but it has always been an important part of Ilongot culture. The Rosaldos learned that headhunting is often connected to an emotion the Ilongot call *liget*. At first the Rosaldos thought that liget meant something like *energized*, but they soon noticed the Ilongot using the word in situations that didn't appear to have anything to do with being energized. They observed that, while feeling liget would sometimes cause members of the tribe to work extremely productively, cutting down many trees in a single day, other times it was connected to a tribe-wide feeling of grief and agitation, which the Ilongot would only be able to assuage through a successful headhunt.

Renato and Michelle lived with the Ilongot only for a year or so. In that time, they observed liget, thought about it, and tried to compare it to their own palette of emotions. They had several theories, none of which seemed to fit. But they gained extensive experience being with people experiencing this emotion.

Years later, on a different project, embedded with a different tribe in a different part of the world, there was an accident. While walking through the forest with some members of this tribe, Michelle accidentally fell off a cliff and died.

Renato himself tells the story on the podcast *Invisibilia* to the host, Alix Spiegel:

**RENATO:** We saw Shelly's body. The feeling I had was just almost a cosmic heaving, expanding and contracting, expanding and contracting, expanding and contracting. But it wasn't just me. It was everything around me.

**SPIEGEL:** That day, crouching next to Shelly's body on the riverbank, he says the seed of an alien emotion he'd never experienced before began to grow inside him. It was muted at first, didn't fully express itself until after, after Renato had flown back to America and arranged the funeral. Then one sunny California afternoon, when he was driving down a highway in Palo Alto, he couldn't bear the pressure. So he pulled over on the side of the road and this sound came roaring out of him.

**RENATO:** I, out of nowhere, just started howling [he demonstrates].

**SPIEGEL:** He felt this feeling in his body was *liget*. And he finally had English words for it.

**RENATO:** It's like being in high voltage.

**SPIEGEL:** High voltage - those are the English words that most closely approximate the feeling of liget.

**RENATO:** Like high voltage was flowing through my body.

Renato realized that this feeling, this emotion, matched every situation he and Michelle had observed in which the Ilongot were feeling liget. It might arise on its own, sort of like that antsy feeling we get sometimes that makes us want to be productive—to go out and do something, *anything*—but it also arrives in otherwise subdued situations of grief and loss, because of connection to loved ones.

And it wasn't until two things converged—a complex and overwhelming life situation sufficient to provoke an extreme physical response, and enough *observation* of liget in other people (similar to the way we tell stories to our children over and over)—that Renato was able to experience liget within himself.

We can see from this example that emotions, like vision, are things we learn to construct. We feel them more keenly, more robustly, when we observe others expressing them. They are a kind of story that members of a culture tell together.

When I look at emotions this way, it becomes obvious how we are using them. I sit in a theater, watching a sad movie, knowing that everyone else in the audience is sharing a feeling inside their body with me. In that moment, I am connected to them. We are the same. It's that connection that strengthens a culture, a people. It's that strength that allows us to continue to exist. Shared emotions like this are, perhaps, the deep thing we all agree on that allows us to overcome our differences and work through conflict together, toward a common goal.

But we are moving toward a global culture, one that values diversity and individuality. How, in such a culture, are we to find that deep, common, shared thing which can make us all feel like one people, despite the fact that we are so obviously different on the surface—and, as we learn more about indigenous peoples' breadth of experiences and expressions of being human, also so very different on the inside?

What is that subtle thing the framers of American independence were talking about when they said "all men are created equal?" We can clearly see this is not true. Obviously, everyone is different. We are not just different heights and shapes and colors, but different hopes and dreams and languages. More than that, even; we have different social constructs, different stories, which produce in us wildly different ways of perceiving reality. And in difference lies the unknown. And in the unknown lies fear. And from fear comes conflict. And finally, conflict, large or small, is the great spreader of suffering. (5.2)

What is the way out of this cycle? Is there a solution to this problem that has plagued humanity for all time, literally since humanity has existed? More importantly, if there isn't a solution —or if we're too shortsighted or weak or afraid to take hold of it —do we deserve to continue to exist? This is, here and now, evolution at work! We are still subject to its forces every moment, just as we are subject to gravity. I think it should be obvious by now that we cannot kill our way to peace.

---

5.2 The framers' own use of the word "men" instead of "people," as well as the fact that many of them were slave owners, suggests they themselves may have had a few things to learn about everyone being equal. I sometimes wonder what moral flaws future generations will look back on us as having. Certainly there will be some we are completely oblivious to.

Even those brave ones who have taken the more noble path of sacrificing themselves for others—Socrates, Jesus, Maximilian Kolbe, Thich Quang Duc, Martin Luther King Jr., and many others—have shown us, tragically, that the juggernaut of suffering is not one that can be stopped by individual acts of courage.

It seems that, if there is a solution, it can only be found in the collective action of each of us. In other words, that you and I, the two people here right now, are the ones responsible for reducing, and hopefully someday eliminating, suffering. And it will not be a grand, heroic act that we must do. No, it is in the small choices we make in each moment. Because suffering is not something that happens on a grand scale—even though we often think about it that way. No, suffering is something that happens inside our own small experience of being.

It feels, as I write this section, that I am allowing us to get distracted from the issue at hand. I started this chapter trying to point out two things to you: that emotions are not what we generally think they are, and that love is not an emotion in any case. I made most of my case for the first point. We can see, based on our examples of the apple and liget, that emotions should be viewed more as constructions than as momentary feelings. The follow-on effect of looking at emotions this way is important: it gives us some measure of control over our emotions. It means that we are not mindless creatures, driven by our feelings. Or, rather, that we are only such mindless creatures as we allow ourselves to be. When we fail to be mindful.

But, suddenly, before I got to the second point, I fell into this hole about suffering. I considered rewriting and reorganizing things, but I think there's something valuable to be found down here. That, in fact, it may be through an examination of the role suffering plays in our lives that we are able to see what love really is.

So let's roll with this for a moment, keeping in mind that

there is a nearby point about the nature of love, but that we must stick around this place, discussing suffering for a bit. I feel confident we will soon discover where these two points meet.

So, recall now that suffering isn't just pain. Suffering is that feeling of *what is happening should NOT be happening*. It is that feeling of wrongness, of denial, of cringing away from the source of the pain, even after the pain has gone. Suffering, in other words, is a response. It is an attempt to reject what *is* by dint of effort, through sheer will. It happens when we get so dogmatically attached to the perspective-bound way we perceive things that we refuse to accept the reality that those things are changing.

But *changing* is simply what reality *is*. You and I are just little beings, caught up in massive currents. Again and again, we forget this, and struggle against the current, refusing to accept what is and trying to change it, only to find ourselves once again violently swept away, tumbled about, disoriented and hurt and no better off than when we started. Except, perhaps, in that we've had another chance to learn our lesson—our lesson about letting go.

As an exercise in letting go, let's switch over, for a moment, to our other converging point: the one about what love is. I remember the first time I thought about this. I was in college, having a conversation with a girlfriend, and we were talking about falling in and out of love with someone. She was arguing that this was just something that happened—but that when you found the right person, after hopelessly falling in love with them, you would know, somehow, that you would never fall out of love with them. The feeling would just be too strong.

I couldn't articulate it very well at the time, but something in me rebelled against this idea. It was incongruous. If falling in love was something we had no control over, then falling out of love must also be. And that would make the idea of any long-term committed relationship absurd. If I wake up next to someone one morning and realize I've fallen in love with them, then there is nothing—*nothing*—to say that one far-off morning in the future I won't wake up next to them and realize I've fallen out of love. We aren't in control of our feelings. We don't know where they'll take us.

No, I thought. This feeling of infatuation we're all familiar with can't be love. But I didn't know anything more about it at that time. It was only years later that I came across the story of the Rosaldos and liget, and began to consider that love, like all complex emotions, might just be a narrative.

And what if it was? Would it solve the problem I was feeling, deep in my intuition? Would love-as-a-narrative be strong enough to fix all the brokenness in the world? To end all the suffering?

I am struggling to write this section. I suspect it's because I have come to a place where I am encountering one of my deepest beliefs. I can't proceed using logic and reason, because I am to some extent working backward from my beliefs, using my logic and reason to justify them. And I am very aware of the fact that, if you don't share my beliefs, no amount of logic and reason will convince you that what I'm saying is at all sensible.

Sensible. Ah, perhaps this word will prove helpful to us here. Look at it: sensible. Sense-able. Able to be sensed. We use the terms sense and nonsense to refer to things that follow logical paths in our thinking. But we also use the term sense to refer to things we perceive in the world. And remember, our beliefs come from our perceptions of the world. So I believe in gravity because I sense gravity. I believe in my coffee mug because I can feel it, here, in my hand. Heck, I believe in my hand because I can feel it there at the end of my arm. These things are sense-able to me.

The belief I am aware of as I write this section is sensible to me. The belief is this: I am loved. That's it. It feels right. It feels true. It feels like I am loved. I sense it. I am loved.

But in conversations with other people, I have often been

told this is not sensible to everyone. This, to me, feels tragic. It feels impossible. It feels like nonsense. It's the same kind of nonsense as if I were feeling gravity while everyone else was floating around, bouncing off of things, unable to connect with the earth, stuck spinning their wheels, tractionless. "Can't you feel it?" I would shout up to them, floating above my head. "Gravity is *right here*! It's not imaginary! It's not nonsense!"

Of course you are loved. I am loved, and I am not special. I am not different than you. You are not different than me. We are the same, the same kind of consciousness. The same Observer. This is why Big Idea #2 is important. This is why, when we fall into the pit of suffering we were examining a moment ago, we know that we are feeling the same thing, just like we're feeling the same gravity. And this is why the question of why I feel that I am loved while other people don't is so important to me. Because when you feel loved, your suffering is lessened. Softened. You can begin to see past the suffering, around it, to the pain itself. No, not the pain—the wound. Whatever it is. Abuse. An angry parent. Being made fun of at school. Not living up to someone else's expectations. A missed opportunity. A loved one dying prematurely. Rejection. Loss. Failure. All these and more, just the different kinds of wounds we receive moving through life.

When you feel loved, you can see that these wounds aren't your fault. You didn't get them because you were bad. You got them because you exist—because you are a real conscious being inside a real reality. You don't deserve to suffer because of these wounds, and when you learn how to see that the wounds don't say anything at all about your goodness, or your worthiness, or your quality as a person—that they're just wounds, the same as a stubbed toe you might swear about but would never take personally—then you can tend to them, the same as you would that stubbed toe, or a cut finger. You can clean them out, bandage them up, and let them be. Let them go. And you can discover, again and again, that, when cared for, wounds heal with time.

I have come to see this healing as an expression of reality's love for me. Because despite my wounds, despite my scars, despite all the weird things about me, I still fit within reality. I still belong. Perhaps not in all places, or at all times, or among all people, but I fit here, in this moment. It's like we discussed earlier, when gazing out over the forest, closely inspecting the tree, or just sitting here, now, with this book in your hands. I take a deep breath, and I know that I exist. And I know that I am loved.

But what if you don't know that? What if you do feel adrift? What if you can't sense this thing I am telling you is so eminently sensible (sense-able)?

Well, then, we're right back where we were, aren't we? In that hole of suffering, talking about what love is, like it's somewhere out there and not inside us. Trying to figure out where these two paths converge—the path of suffering and the path of love. But I hope that now, you have a sense that I have been on the path of love, and am genuinely trying to explain to you how to get to it.

But, before I explain, I want you to know one thing. I hope you can hear it, deep inside, at the level of your belief, with your Observer's perception. It is this:

I love you.

There. That's it. That's why I've written this book. It's for you. It's to tell you I love you. If you can hear that, if you believe it deep down, you could stop right now. You got the point. You got the message: I love you.

But if you're having trouble believing how some stranger could say that to you, could make the apparently ridiculous claim that he loves you and wrote this book to you, for you, without even knowing who you are, well... maybe I could finish telling you what I think love is?

Let's start with the biggest story.

Somewhere around 13.8 billion years ago, something exploded. We don't really know what it was, or what caused it, or even if "explosion" is the best term for it. We just know the evidence suggests this happened. This explosion, which we quaintly call the Big Bang, was the start of what looks like everything.

A few seconds after the explosion, everything was pretty hot. As things tend to be following explosions. But they started cooling down because, you know, heat dissipates. Whatever. The science of it is far beyond me. I'm just telling the story.

Eventually, all the hot stuff cooled down enough that it started forming into patterns. One pattern, by far the most common one, apparently, is what we today call *hydrogen*. There was a whole lot of hydrogen. It was a pretty stable pattern.

The thing about hydrogen is that it has mass, and there's something about mass that attracts other stuff with mass. Today, we call this something *gravity*. Gravity got to work on all the hydrogen, and in fairly short order it was all clumped together. As it clumped together, the forces we today call *pressure* and *friction* and probably some other ones I don't understand caused the hydrogen at the center of the big clump to mash together and fuse into a new pattern that we today call *helium*. This continuously exploding/burning clump of hydrogen and helium we today call a *star*.

Gravity continued to work on all the stars that had formed, clumping them, in turn, together into what we call *galaxies*. Galaxies collide. Stars crash into each other and explode. Stars burn up all their hydrogen fuel and collapse or explode, depending on how big they are. Exploded stars cause *nebulae* to form, which are clouds of gas somewhat similar to the cloud of gas that existed right after the Big Bang. New stars form in nebulae, and as hydrogen and helium continue to be smashed together and burned, smashed and burned, heavier and heavier elements are created. It's all very spectacularly chaotic. Lots of smashing and explosions and destruction.

Anyway, the heavier elements, hurtling through the void, are eventually captured by the biggest gravity wells—stars. These spinning conglomerations of material slowly clump together themselves, forming molten globs of rock and metal, or huge blobs of gas that don't have quite enough mass to themselves ignite into new stars. These blobs of rock and gas, orbiting their particular stars, become *planets*. The groupings of stars and planets are what we today call *solar systems*.

One particular solar system, in one particular galaxy, had one particular planet with a lot of different kinds of substances. As it cooled, many of these substances eventually got to the right temperature where they were all sort of suspended together in this liquid soup. All the substances were swirling around in the soup, bumping into each other and, on occasion, sticking. These stuck-together substances are what we today call *molecules*. At some point, something happened that caused some of the molecules in that soup to start replicating themselves. They were stable enough to exist without falling apart, but complex enough to grab material from the soup and make exact copies of themselves. This process of high-fidelity molecular replication we today call *life*.

Everything I described in the above seven paragraphs took something like 11.2 billion of what we now call *years* to occur.

Over the next couple billion years, the replicating molecules slowly got more and more complex. Today we call these more complex life forms *bacteria* and *algae*. They started doing things like harvesting energy from sunlight, or consuming other life forms and breaking their molecules down for energy.

About 900 million years ago, some of these life forms evolved different parts of themselves, each of which performed different necessary tasks that aided in the organism's survival. These different types of *cells* would eventually become what we today call *organs*.

About 540 million years ago, something seems to have happened that caused the number and complexity of life forms to rapidly increase. Today we call this period the *Cambrian explosion*. Some animals became capable of absorbing denser elements and used them to construct the cells of rigid *skeletal systems*, which enabled them to become much more mobile and resilient.

From here, the already-accelerating timeline of our story really begins to take off.

By about 440 million years ago, some of these skeletal creatures had moved out of the water and onto dry land.

400 million years ago saw the appearance of the first four-legged animals.

300 million years ago heralded the arrival of predator species, adapted to consuming not just plant matter, but other animals.

250 million years ago and we had dinosaurs.

200 million years and we had mammals.

66 million years ago saw the mass extinction that seems likely to have been caused by an asteroid impact. This event was particularly hard on the cold-blooded reptiles, and warm-blooded mammals, able to regulate their temperature more flexibly, began to prosper and adapt to the new environment. Within 16 million years there were all kinds of apes and monkeys, the predecessors of anatomically modern humans.

The subsequent 49 million years or so heralded the rise of *megafauna*—giant versions of mammals like sloths, bears, tigers, and some species that still exist today: elephants, rhinoceroses, giraffes, and others, most of which only exist on the plains of the landmass we now call *Africa*.

It was only 500,000 years ago that the first anatomically modern humans appeared in Africa. 380,000 years later they spread out of Africa. Several subspecies came into existence, but were later—perhaps through subsequent dispersals from Africa —eliminated through violence or absorbed through interbreeding (or a mix of both) into what we today call *Homo Sapiens*, which is us.

Quite the heritage.

By about 40,000 years ago, humans had spread (by some accounts a second time) from Africa to the entirety of the *Eurasian* continent—including the *Pacific Islands* and *Australia*.

Estimates vary, but it seems to have been about 12,000 years ago that humans first arrived in what we today call the *Americas*.

This is about the time of the dawn of what we today call *history*—of humans passing their perspective-based narratives down through the generations. We got *agriculture* in the Levant, a method of more efficiently converting land resources into human food. Agriculture gave rise to *cities* and *nations*, and advanced technologies like metal smelting. Ideas such as *currency* developed, allowing people to work together more flexibly. Large and powerful nations arose in both the East and the West and were largely isolated from one another for several thousand years.

And the rest, well, you probably know from your schooling. How those ancient empires spread their influence and ideas, rightly or wrongly, through history to this very day, where they still influence you and me.

At each point in this narrative, an unimaginably complex interconnected set of things interacted in practically infinite ways to produce the reality that you and I are experiencing right now. Not just the language you're reading this book in, or the language I wrote it in (which may or may not be the same language), but the keyboard I type it on, which is arranged based on the ape hands my ancestors evolved, which is based on the demands of the environment. The materials my hands are made of—bone and muscle and tendon and skin—come from the same raw materials that were available in the primordial soup, and those materials were forged in the heart of long-dead stars, and accreted into the planet we now call *Earth*. Each moment of the last 13.8 billion years has contributed to the existence of this one. It is an unbroken chain of causality stretching back in the mists of time as far as we can see. I certainly wouldn't say it was deliberately working *just* to produce me, or this moment in my life. But I would definitely say it eventually *succeeded* in doing so.

And the same is true of you, and this moment in your life.

So let's look at one more piece of this puzzle before we start to draw all these threads together. So far we have suffering, love, and the history of the universe. The fourth thread we have to draw on is the evidence.

Earlier we talked about how we use the word love in so many different contexts: sex, partnership, friends, family, children, food, activities, and more. Now, I'm not sure if that's a fluke of language or if there's actually something consistent across all those things. But, if there *was* something consistent, then it stands to reason that we should be able to find some *evidence* of it.

I've given this a lot of thought. What is consistent across all those areas? Enjoyment? Well, not always. We often struggle mightily through massive amounts of conflict with those we love. Something continues to bring us back to them, even when we know we won't enjoy it. So it can't be enjoyment.

Is it survival? Merely evolution pushing our buttons to try to get us to do things that are good for us? Again, not always. We often choose to sacrifice things we know will be good for us for the sake of the people and things we love. Love definitely doesn't always seem to be pushing us toward survival and spreading our genes.

Is it goodwill? Once again, that doesn't seem quite right. There are plenty of times we go out of our way to say or do something hurtful to those we love.

Well, if the evidence is there, it's certainly not easy to see. In fact, this sort of trial-and-error pondering might not ever get us to the point where we recognize the thing that's right in front of us. It's not how I arrived at a knowledge of the evidence, anyway. In fact, I don't even remember when I realized it. I think I must have stumbled across it while writing an earlier draft of this book.

I'll spare you the rest of the dramatic tension and just tell you what seems to be present whenever and wherever we say we love something: effort. It's effort. We are always *trying* on behalf of the things we love. *Trying* to spend time with them. *Trying* to connect with them. *Trying* to get more of them. *Trying* to help them. *Trying* to prevent their suffering. *Trying* to set them free. Even *trying*, sometimes, to push their buttons or drive them crazy. The evidence of love is *trying*.

And once I realized this, I quickly noticed that you can turn it around, too. That wherever there is effort, wherever there is trying, there is probably love nearby.

And now the threads come together, and the puzzle pieces lock in place: because where else has the most time and energy, the most effort, the most *trying*, gone into but this present moment? Reality has been cooking up this present moment for the last 13.8 billion years. All the work of the Big Bang, and friction, and gravity, and inertia, and heat transfer went into producing the stars and the galaxies and the solar systems of the universe. All the work of chemistry went into producing complex molecules, capable of replicating themselves. All the work of molecular biology went into complexifying those molecules to the point where we considered them to be alive. All the work of photosynthesis and evolutionary biology and random point mutations went into producing the astonishingly beautiful forest of life across the history of Earth. All the work of thinking and culture and creativity went into the spreading of human beings across the face of the earth. All the work of freedom and justice and morality and philosophy have brought us to this point in time, with this mind of ours, able to perceive this reality we share using an Observer parked behind the eyes of a brilliant and beautiful variety of ape. And not only to perceive it, but to describe it, to revel in it, to shape it, to share it, to dance with it. To love it.

This moment, right here and right now, is the culmination of all the work reality has ever done. All the effort. All the trying. All the love.

No, love isn't an emotion. Far from it. Love is a force of the universe, working to bring this moment, and all moments, into existence. Working, perhaps, toward order—or if not that, then some other vast goal far beyond my little human comprehension.

Now, it may be easy for us to scoff at the idea, since reality is just an unconscious thing. But is it? This, in fact, is the whole reason I took the time to go through Big Idea #1. Reality is just one thing, and you and I are part of it.

And if I am part of reality, and I love you, then reality loves you at least to the extent that I do. That's basic transitive thinking. The fact that this book exists and you are reading it is evidence that reality loves you.

And who knows what was around 10 billion years ago, before we were? Are there other consciousnesses out in the universe? Are there things we haven't yet encountered or even imagined? It would be foolish to think there aren't. Remember Big Idea #1 and its offshoot: we don't know anything. We are proved wrong every day—and not just us, but even our best and brightest scientists. It's all far too big for us to know. What was around before the Big Bang? Perhaps it was a consciousness of some sort. Just like my Observer. Just like yours.

And if that's too difficult for you to accept, if that's not sense-able to you, then you need look no further than the fact that you're here, now, right now in this moment. And, whether or not you've been aware of it, that's been true your whole life. So, in other words, for your whole life you've always been *trying* to continue to exist. You've been an active collaborator with reality to get here, to this moment. That's taken a great deal of effort on your part. And effort is evidence of love. So it seems clear that, even if you can't see it all the time, you love yourself. You've loved yourself, perhaps all the way from your moment of conception, into this very moment, right now.

The suffering gets in the way of that. Earlier I said we were in a hole of suffering, and that's a good metaphor for what it's like. No matter what direction we look, all we see is suffering. But when we can realize that the love is there—our love for ourselves, our love for others, and reality's love for us—then we can take a deep breath, let go of the attachment or the clinging or the fear or whatever it is that's causing the pain to become suffering, and we can once again feel that love.

If love is some kind of universal force, then when you feel it, it isn't just a feeling. It's you touching something real. It's exactly the same kind of thing as when I feel the table beneath my hand. The table is real, and I know this because I can sense it. So, too, love is real, and I know this because I can sense it.

It seems to me that the one thing that requires the smallest amount of belief is to believe that you exist. (I, too, believe you exist.) And because you exist, and have existed for your whole life, then so far, the very things you needed must have always been right there to be had. Because you're here, aren't you? Here in this moment? You made it! You're alive, being carried into the future by love. It isn't always easy. Quite the opposite, in fact; love promises us effort, not ease. But every bit of effort, no matter how small it might seem to you, is another piece of evidence piled onto the enormous mountain of evidence that you are loved. I am as sure of this as I am of anything: if you can't see it or feel it, all you need to do is keep searching, keep asking, keep trying. The proof is in the fact that you keep going. Just as you have been doing your whole life. Just as you will continue to do for the rest of it.

And when the time comes to set the burden down, to do what we call *die*, I don't claim to know what will happen. Anyone who does is making things up, probably to assuage their own fear of the unknown. But it makes sense to me—and so I believe—that since every moment of my Observer's existence that my thinker can remember has so far been the same, passing from one moment to the next, watching reality go by, then death will be more of the same. Just one more bump in the road into whatever future reality has in store for me.

Hey. How are you feeling?

I'm feeling a little tender. A little sad. I get this way whenever I think about death. But in a very real way, that sadness, that tenderness, is what prompted me to write this book.

You see, for many years after I lost my Christian faith, I just lived up in my head. Up in my thinker. This is when I became the most skeptical version of myself. I like thinking. I'm good at thinking. So I didn't pay Attention to my feelings very often, because feelings aren't rational, just like faith isn't rational. Of course, in the throes of my skepticism I couldn't see the actual problem: I was hurt. My feelings were hurt pretty badly. I felt like I'd been betrayed.

Skepticism became a refuge for me, a way to ignore my pain while it slowly, slowly healed. Of course, in the throes of my skepticism, I couldn't see this. I thought I was just being oh-so rational. But eventually, my hurt feelings had healed enough that they were ready for me to start reconnecting with them. But I wasn't able to notice, stuck as I was in my dogmatic skepticism.

I lived like this for years. Looking back on that time, the cost of too much skepticism is clear: I was unable to connect. To people, to life. To myself. It was a period of my life full of a lot of unacknowledged suffering—and I exported far too much of it to the people who were in my life: friends, coworkers, girlfriends.

My strong emotions around death were the thing that eventually jarred me loose from this sort of numb half-existence. I remember the moment. I was in a coffee shop, interviewing a woman about a business she had started. She told me she had gone on a vision quest, and had learned that she was meant to work with death and dying. Something sparked in my emotions; some sadness and pain about my mortality, yes, but also some curiosity. From there, I began searching. And have since discovered (or rediscovered) every single idea I've shared with you in this book.

Earlier I told you that I love you. I remember an instance, several years ago, while I was still getting comfortable with all this stuff. One of my teachers, whom I had just had coffee with, told me he loved me as we were saying goodbye. I remember being struck by that. Not weirded out, exactly, but unsure of how to respond. It felt unfamiliar for someone not in my family or a close friend to say that. I honestly don't remember what I said in response. But I think now, today, I am able to hear what he meant. It's the same thing I expressed just a little while ago.

Part of the difficulty in hearing and accepting that we're loved has to do with the idea of deservingness. A lot of people think they don't deserve love. They think they are bad, or stupid, or worthless. But these are just wounds that have been inflicted on their thinker. Maybe you can relate?

I have a little thought exercise I like to do when I'm feeling like I don't deserve to be loved. I'll walk you through it now:

Photo by Zak Boca on Unsplash

That's a pretty majestic waterfall. Beautiful. Awe-inspiring, even.

Unfortunately, the photographer disagrees. He thinks the framing and color saturation are all wrong. He doesn't like the focus, he bungled the rule of threes, and if he had been patient and waited just a few more hours he would have gotten a clear blue sky to really make the edge of the cliff pop.

(Note that I made these criticisms up for the purposes of my argument; I don't actually know what Zak Boca thinks of his photograph.)

But look at the distinction that's being missed here. A picture is two things: a thing, in itself; and a depiction of that thing.

Imagine the photographer saying the same things about the Seljalandsfoss waterfall that he said about his photograph of it:

"That waterfall's color saturation is all wrong."

"It's out of focus."

"It should be falling off the cliff a little closer to the camera. That would be optimally majestic."

These are absurd things to say about a waterfall. The waterfall is what it is. It's perfect. There's nothing wrong with it. It's exactly how it's supposed to be, if it even makes sense to say that waterfalls are "supposed to be." They just *are*. Loved into existence by millions of years of effort.

Remember this: in exactly the same way a photograph is a description of a waterfall, your identity is just a description of your self. Identity is just a story we tell. For example, Michael Marvosh isn't real. And, just like the photograph of the waterfall, he isn't perfect. He's got a ton of flaws. He fails all the time. He has enough personal and personality issues to work on for the rest of his life.

But the actual human being we're talking about when we say Michael Marvosh, that one is like the waterfall. A body, mind, and spirit, brought into existence by the universe. Just existing, exactly as he was meant to be.

The same is true of you. There is nothing lacking in you. Not a single hair out of place. You are perfect, just the way you are.

And we can keep that in mind at the same time that we're aware of our absurdly flawed identities. And when we do, it helps us realize that we can love them, too. We can have compassion for their limits and shortcomings.

Michael Marvosh, the identity, is just a tool my thinker and Observer have collaborated to construct. He's the best we could do. Sometimes we get angry at him, or roll his eyes at the dumb things he does. But we know that he's trying, and we, in turn, are trying to help him learn from his mistakes. And that trying is evidence of love, both directed at him and proceeding from him.

You and I probably haven't met in person. Michael Marvosh probably doesn't know your identity. So when I say I love you, I am speaking, first and foremost, from my Observer to your Observer. From waterfall to waterfall. But, in all honesty, I am also speaking from my Observer to your identity, from waterfall to photograph. I know you aren't perfect. No one is. But I bet you've tried your best. And I hope you keep trying.

I love you. I love that you exist. I hope you continue to exist. And I think reality loves you, too. And I hope that my words here help you learn to love yourself. I hope you grow, and learn, and thrive. But most of all I hope you keep trying. I hope you continue to love. That is my wish for you. That is my wish for all things.

You can love yourself because reality loves you. You don't need to be perfect or deserving. In fact, you can't be. Your identity is always going to be a patch-job, the result of your Observer and thinker doing the best they could do in a limited situation, staggering from whatever wounds you happened to receive— especially during your childhood—learning from other people's identities who are equally wounded and flawed. That's just part of what it means to be human.

When we learn to see things from this perspective, we can then learn to see that all our suffering, unpleasant as it may be, is just pain we are holding onto, instead of allowing it to be what it is, in this temporary moment, which will soon pass.

And as we get better and better at letting go of our own

suffering, we will inflict less and less pain on those around us. And as we inflict less and less pain, they will have more and more opportunity to notice that their suffering, too, is self-inflicted.

And this is the simple way in which love can heal the world. There's nothing grand about it. It's really quite humble. It's only each of us doing our own work. Trying to see clearly. Recognizing when we aren't doing our best, and trying to correct ourselves. Learning from our mistakes, rather than blaming ourselves (or others) for them. Just allowing ourselves to be, and helping others to be.

What would a world full of such loving people look like? I don't know. I suspect it would be a world with a lot less fear and judgment, and a lot more cooperation and problem solving. Whatever it would end up looking like, I'd really like to see it. And I'm trying to do my part.

I hope you join me, you brilliant and beautiful waterfall of a human being.

So that's all I have to say about love for now. The next chapter of the book is about one always-useful thing we can do in response to these three Big Ideas.

# CHAPTER SIX
# CONCLUSION: PAY ATTENTION!

So...

What? *So what?* What's the point?

This is what I imagine some people saying.

*So what* if reality is all one thing and we can only describe it but not understand it? *So what* if you are a perspective-bound consciousness that often confuses itself with its human identity? *So what* if reality loves us and we learn to love ourselves and others? It's not going to *fix* anything. All of this is so *impractical*.

Or maybe your response is on the other end of the spectrum. Maybe you're feeling sort of overwhelmed by... all of it. By both the magnitude of this truth I'm trying to point to, and the way it touches your life, personally, uniquely, each and every moment.

Well, both responses are understandable—as well as those between. I myself fall somewhere on the spectrum between them every day. Sometimes I feel connected to everything, in awe of all the love that's brought me to this present moment, content with myself and my life; other times I feel like I'm drowning in problems, spellbound by the narrative and unable to see a way out other than to suffer through. The challenge is that we need our stories to survive, even when it seems they may be distracting us from the very point of living.

It's almost as if there are two modes we can be in as human beings. One of them is akin to gazing out over the forest: we sense the Whole, the Unity, God or the Universe or Reality or whatever you want to call it. The other mode is like encountering a tree while wandering lost: road-weary, aware of only the problem before us and trying to navigate around it with a minimum of stumbles and scrapes.

Life can often feel only like the second mode. Overcoming challenge after challenge until you're numb with exhaustion and monotony. Wake up, eat, go to work, come home, eat, sleep. Do it all again tomorrow. In an attempt to separate one monotony from another, we created vacations and weekends. But, inevitably, we return to the plodding grind of moving from one tree to the next, to the next. Even our weekends and vacations start to feel monotonous and stressful. We know the forest is "out there," but there's no point in thinking about it because it doesn't help us make it past this next tree.

What a perfect trap we're in! The story—the very thing that enables us to do all the things we're doing—is also the curse that traps us in an endless loop of doing them. What is the way out? How do we escape this maze of tree after tree after tree?

One answer to that question is inevitable: death. It's a challenging answer for all kinds of reasons. It's not the reason I want to highlight in this book, but it would be irresponsible of me not to discuss it.

Some people suffer so greatly that they just want out. They just want to not be here anymore. The only permanent solution to the problem of being trapped (as far as we can tell, anyway) is death. A longing for death is one understandable response to great suffering. Trying to empathize with that tragic feeling is itself a kind of suffering. I don't wish that much pain on anyone. No one deserves it. No one asked to be put here in this existence.

We all just showed up one day and are expected to do our best, despite the fact that we all fail.

I had a close friend whose response to the suffering was alcohol. He was a brilliant person. An expert designer, a connector of people, a teller of stories. His laugh filled up a room. He was the life of the party. Yet in those quiet times between, he was apparently tormented by something he couldn't figure out how to share, nor how to set down. And the medicine he found that eased his suffering was alcohol. It eventually killed him. He just got sick and his body wasn't strong enough to recover. It was devastating, not just to me, but to his parents and his siblings and all his friends. We all loved him so dearly. It just seems like he couldn't see past whatever pain he was going through. I still miss Eric. I miss him every day. And I hope that, if he still exists somewhere out there, that he's found the comfort he was looking for.

It's a hard lesson to accept, that death is one way out of the suffering of life. It's certainly not an easy way. Many people try to deny it, to not talk about it. I suspect we think that if we talk about it, more people will be liable to choose that way out earlier than they otherwise would come to it naturally. I don't know if that's true, though. I think it's probably better to always try to tell the truth—maybe especially when it's difficult. I never really talked to Eric about his drinking and what it was doing to him, and I sometimes wonder what might have happened if I had. It's easy to play these kinds of "what if" games with ourselves. They, too, are another tree, another obstacle in our path for us to find our way around.

Happily, death is not the only way to escape the suffering of wandering lost amongst the trees of your life.

To see the other way out, we must come back to the question we began this section with: what is the point? What is the point of being alive? What is the point of living?

We ask that question as if there's an answer we can fully

understand. But it's an absurd question. A point is a small thing —the smallest imaginable thing, really. If we want to know what point our lives have, we need to view them as points—as tiny occurrences within the vast ocean of time and space. How could we comprehend the point of our lives from that scope? Perhaps our lives have a point on a cosmic scale—but they don't have a point to us. To us, our lives are long. From our perspective, we are less like trees, and more like forests of experience.

And yet, when we earnestly ask "where am I?" within that forest of experience, the answer is always the same: right here, in this moment. This moment, this single tree of your existence, is the only thing you will ever have. Yes, you can look back on your past and see the forest, and you can imagine looking forward into your future and seeing a forest there, too, but those forests exist only in this single moment, called the present, where you always find yourself. Whenever you stop to look, you are here, next to this tree, in this moment. The forest you think of as your past exists only in this moment, as you recall it. The forest you imagine will be your future exists only in this moment, as a story you tell. And so while it may be true that your life is a forest and this moment only a tree, it is also true, just as with the infinite recursive complexity of reality itself, that the forest is the tree. That your life, such as it is, is only happening right now. Right as you read these words. And when you set this book down and return to your family or friends, to your job or your home, or to whatever situation awaits you (and the stories you tell yourself about it), that moment will be your life. Life isn't a collection of moments. It's just one moment, one tree, stretching backward in memory and forward in imagination. Nobody knows what it is, even while we all live it. What a strange thing!

So the point of life, as far as I can tell, is simple. It's not to understand, or to figure it out. The point is the thing every cat knows, and the thing we all used to know when we were infants, but forgot when we learned to speak. The point of life is just this: *to be alive.*

And the follow-on realization here is that the way out of suffering is simply to see your suffering in this context. As one moment in an ever-changing sea, just a moment that is passing by, as have all the other moments of your life, as will all the rest of the moments yet to come.

And the way to do that is by practicing what we'll be talking about for the rest of this book: paying close Attention to this moment as it passes by.

We did this exercise a little earlier, so it should be at least a bit familiar to you. Right now, in this moment, you are sitting, or lying down. If you're walking or running or driving, stop for a moment. Pull over to the side of the road if you have to. Seriously, try it. It will take literally two minutes. But in order to benefit from this, you need to pause and spend those minutes noticing. In other words, pay Attention. I'm asking you to pay Attention.

Now that you're settled, *first* read the entire next paragraph, and only *after* having fully read it, *then* close your eyes and follow its instructions.

First, breathe in, and notice the expansion of your chest and belly. Feel the air moving into you. Breathe out, and notice the collapse of your chest and belly. Feel the air relaxing out of you. Repeat the inhale and exhale. Breathe slowly, deliberately, calmly. Take five full, deep breaths this way, then open your eyes. Got it? Five breaths, Attention on how they feel. Ready? Ok, then close your eyes and do it. Go.

Now that you've calmed your nervous system a bit and focused your Attention, try to maintain that slow awareness of your breath, and spend one minute looking around you. Notice the room you're in—and your place in it. Notice the position of your body on whatever you are sitting or lying or standing on. Notice how it feels. See how the light illuminates the space. Feel the temperature of the air. Pay Attention to whatever your Attention is drawn to nearby or in your body. Don't narrate in your mind. Just observe. Continue for a minute or so, until you notice your mind has wandered from the moment, and you're thinking about something else. Then come back here.

Ok, if you were walking or running or driving, feel free to carefully resume that activity. Be aware of your surroundings.

Now, the exercise you just did is an exercise in what is often called mindfulness. It's a very old idea, which can be found in many of our most enduring books. Mindfulness is talked about in the Buddhist sutras and Hindu scriptures as well as, to a lesser extent, those of Judaism, Christianity, and Islam; and in philosophical writings from Eastern and, again to a lesser extent, Western traditions. Mindfulness has been taught throughout the centuries by gurus and monks, and more recently popularized as part of yoga practices, and even by nonreligious thinkers and writers such as Eckhart Tolle.

Even though I really like the exercise we just did, I don't really like the term mindfulness. I disagree with the word "mind" in this context, because I think our minds are things we construct over the course of our lives—primarily throughout our childhood. A mind isn't something we were born with, like a foot or an elbow. ( And I've never heard of anyone practicing "footfulness" or "elbowfulness.") Once again, we need imagine nothing more unusual than a newborn infant to see this. A newborn infant has a brain, certainly, and with that brain a consciousness. Infants seem to be aware of themselves and their surroundings. But I wouldn't say a newborn has a mind yet. They don't have words, and while they definitely have experiences, they aren't yet capable of expressing those experiences as thoughts. No, a mind is a construction built in large part from language, which is a kind of mental technology we all learned to use within the first few years of our lives.

Think of your mind as something you've built, rather than as something you have innately. It's more like a career than a hand. Attention, on the other hand, is something else. Something deeper. A few moments spent observing a newborn infant should serve to make you completely confident that it has Attention. Few of us can *watch* like a baby watches. Babies are experts at paying Attention. But I don't think they can be mindful.

The second reason I prefer the term paying Attention over mindfulness is, I admit, strategic. I feel that mindfulness is a little overused these days, and that some of my readers might have some baggage attached to it. Maybe you're one of them. If that's the case, my hope in talking about paying Attention instead is to help you set aside whatever negative associations you have with the idea of mindfulness.

If you can see my point about you being, at your core, a conscious awareness, an Observer, then it becomes evident that Attention is where your Observer is directing its awareness. Attention is, therefore, literally the currency of your existence. It's what you choose to spend—or not to spend—in relation to this present moment.

And the better you are at noticing your Attention, and at spending it well, the less you will suffer.

This is true for all kinds of reasons, big and small. We'll go through a few of them in this chapter—in other words, we'll talk about *why* you should pay Attention. (Later, in the Appendix, we'll look at a few exercises you can use to *practice* paying Attention—same as we need to practice anything we want to be good at.)

The first reason to pay Attention is quite common sense: it's good for you. People who are practiced at paying Attention—at being fully present in this moment; at breathing slowly, deeply, and consciously; and at not letting their thoughts get the better of them—have lower blood pressure, more expertly manage their emotions, enjoy richer interpersonal relationships, and are generally (as meditation advocate Dan Harris puts it) "less of an asshole to others."

In short, learning to pay Attention here, now, in this moment or any moment is both a healthy thing to do and makes you a better person.

The second reason to pay Attention is much more esoteric. It is perhaps best expressed in a quote from Buddhist monk Thich Nhat Hanh: "The mind is like a monkey swinging from branch to branch through a forest, says the Sutra. In order not to lose sight of the monkey by some sudden movement, we must watch the monkey constantly and even to be one with it. Mind contemplating mind is like an object and its shadow—the object cannot shake the shadow off. The two are one. Wherever the mind goes, it still lies in the harness of the mind. The Sutra sometimes uses the expression 'Bind the monkey' to refer to taking hold of the mind. But the monkey image is only a means of expression. Once the mind is directly and continually aware of itself, it is no longer like a monkey. There are not two minds, one which swings from branch to branch and another which follows after to bind it with a piece of rope... Once you are able to quiet your mind, once your feelings and thoughts no longer disturb you, at that point your mind will begin to dwell in mind. Your mind will take hold of mind in a direct and wondrous way which no longer differentiates between subject and object. Drinking a cup of tea, the seeming distinction between the one who drinks and the tea being drunk evaporates. Drinking a cup of tea becomes a direct and wondrous experience in which the distinction between subject and object no longer exists."

I fear I have only the faintest glimmer of an understanding of what Nhat Hanh is talking about here, but I'll do my best to untangle it for you. I think he is articulating an ancient expression of what science and Western philosophy have begun to realize within the last hundred years or so: that all our experiences are constructed within our brain—that, in fact, none of what we experience as being reality is actually real. That reality is real, and our experience of it is real. But while our experience may be a real construction of a real reality, it is not reality itself. It's the easiest thing in the world to forget that all we have is this perspective, and not the truth.

The two reasons above come from other mindfulness advocates. The three below are my own, proceeding from the three Big Ideas earlier in the book. I think paying Attention is the most direct and sensible response to our human situation, and those Big Ideas are my best distillation of that situation. So it only makes sense to continue to pull on that thread here in the last chapter of the book.

———

## REASON #1: SO THAT WE CAN IMPROVE OUR UNDERSTANDING

Big Idea #1 is that reality is everything, and that we don't have direct access to it. All we can do is perceive it through our senses and model it in our minds. We are inevitably wrong in our understanding, because our understanding is limited while reality itself seems likely to be unlimited.

Our old religions have a word for when we do something wrong, or bad, or evil. They call it *sin*. Now, I don't believe in sin, exactly, but I do believe that there is a certain kind of thing we can do wrong in regards to Big Idea #1, and when we do this thing wrong, we bring unnecessary suffering into the world.

Remember that Big Idea #1 has to do with how reality is big, unwordsable, and beyond our comprehension. Those things may be true, but reality is not beyond our *perception*. Our senses do render to our consciousness the form reality takes when a human consciousness moves through it. What we perceive is not arbitrary, but a real reflection of real things that really exist. If there is anything good in existence, it must be that which is actually in existence. If living things are to survive and prosper, they will do so by virtue of getting a good enough idea of what's going on within this reality.

That is why, if there is such a thing as evil, I think it must be when we, knowingly or unknowingly, misrepresent our perceptions of reality—in other words, when we lie about what we did, or saw, or think. This is wrong because when we do so, we rob ourselves and others of accurate information about what's going on here. We take from them their ability to make the best possible decision given the situation they're in. Even with good information it's hard enough to make our way through this life. Let's not make it more difficult for others, if we can help it.

True, we can't always help it. In Big Idea #1, I used an example of flat earth and round earth to demonstrate the situation we're in: that everything we think is wrong. So in a way, we can't help but be evil, because we can't perfectly describe reality. This is, perhaps, along the lines of what our old religions call *original* sin. It's a sin of our nature, which we can't escape.

But that is no good excuse to not try to do our best to faithfully and accurately describe what reality looks like to us. The fact that we will inevitably fail to be perfect is an awful reason not to try to be better. On the other hand, it should be easy to have compassion for those who do fail. After all, we have been right where they are. Heck, we're almost certainly failing right in this moment and not even aware of it.

All we can do is our best. And encourage others to do the same. And when we or they mess up, to understand, forgive, and offer another chance. To try to learn from our mistakes, heal from our wounds, and rise from our stumbles. And keep going. That seems to be what life wants from us, given our deep survival instinct.

And what is the one thing that must be present in order for us to give our best account of our perception of reality? Of course it is the very thing we're talking about in this chapter of the book: we must *pay Attention*. Every great lesson we have ever learned about where our understanding of reality is off-base has come when someone has been paying Attention. It happened when Gautama Buddha was sitting under his tree. It happened when the astronomers of ancient Babylon tracked the movements of the planets every night for hundreds of years. It happened when Copernicus realized those very movements were evidence that the sun did not revolve around the earth. It happened when Isaac Newton, again sitting beneath a tree, saw an apple fall to the earth and wondered if a single force was responsible for that apple's falling and the moon remaining in orbit. It happened when Einstein imagined a person falling off a roof and realized that everything is falling forward in time as well as space. It happened when Hawking and Penrose realized that, if our understanding of relativity is accurate, then the universe must have begun as a singularity. Heck, it happened before all those things, before living memory, even, when the first person became aware that a sound could represent something, and the first word was recognized. Yes, any and all human progress, both as individuals, as cultures, as civilizations, as a species, and as a part of reality at any level, has come from paying Attention. Attention is what makes this moment come alive.

The point here, if there is one, is this: when we can pay Attention to the way reality *actually* appears to us, rather than the way we *think* we already understand about how it appears to us, we have a chance to learn more about what's true. We would do better to always be paying Attention—to be open to seeing the ways in which we are wrong.

Let's look at an example of this. Actually, let's reexamine something we discussed earlier, in Big Idea #1. We're going to think again about the idea of flat earth versus round earth.

The idea that, even today, we're probably wrong about the shape of the earth glosses over an important point, which is this: *describing the earth as round is a better description of reality than describing it as flat*. Thinking of the earth as flat is a *regression* to an earlier, less accurate mental model of what the earth looks like. By this point in time, anyone exposed to the evidence that the earth is round should have come to accept it—anyone, that is, who is paying Attention.

The fact that reality is big and incomprehensible is not carte blanche to believe whatever we like. A crucial part of our deep-seated survival imperative is to try to perceive as accurately as possible. And that requires nothing more important than our ability to pay Attention. To try to discern what is and what is not illusion. To use not just our senses, but our consensus. To use not just our language, but our logic. The more tools we can bring to bear on a particular aspect of reality, the more perspectives we can gather on it, and the more we can Attentively let go of our insecure need for *we ourselves to be the one whose perspective is best*; the better will be our understanding of this reality we find ourselves in, the more we will learn, and the better we will survive. And, of course, the better we survive, the more we will be able to learn. It is a cycle, just like all the other cycles of life that surround us. It is when we try to stop the cycle that we get ourselves into trouble—or, on the other hand, when we try to accelerate it faster than it naturally wants to go.

Every human baby is a scientist at heart. You can see it in their actions. Even though they may not be able to explicitly think the words, it's obvious when they throw something on the floor or put something in their mouth that they're thinking, "what happens when I do *this*?" And they pay Attention to the outcome. Oh, how they pay Attention! May we all carry that wonderful trait forward with us into adulthood, and into the future!

Becoming a true adult is recognizing the truth that we are never finished. That the cycle is never complete; that's what makes it a cycle. When we can pay Attention, we can see that we are just one small part in an unimaginable whole, and that the whole is changing, and that we are changing, moment by moment, on and on into the future. Our old religions have a word for it when we cling to things that are dead, finished, and unchanging: *idolatry*. Sometimes we apply the same error to ourselves: when we think of ourselves as grown up, finished products, we idolize ourselves.

This is understandable. As children, we don't have the necessary mental complexity to sense this endless cycle of everything. We imagine our future selves as doctors, or astronauts, or presidents (or, for those of us who will become artists, we imagine ourselves as giraffes or unicorns or clouds). But then when we become those things we so often forget that we are also still the children we once were. That we are not done, not complete. That we are still changing, growing, evolving—and that we will continue to do so until the moment we pass away. Come, let us be adults together! Let us not idolize the versions of ourselves we imagined as children, or berate ourselves for not living up to the dreams we once had. Let us continue to grow and evolve and participate in this ever-changing dance we call life. That is what it means to be an adult: to accept what you are in this moment and to simultaneously realize that you will be, in every moment to come, in the process of becoming.

We can respond to Big Idea #1 in many ways, and we can think of them as being on a spectrum. On the one end we have the regressive response of holding on to old ways of seeing things. This is an attempt to slow the cycle of change. It isn't inherently good or bad, but when we're paying Attention we can see it for what it is, rather than choose it as the knee-jerk reaction we're most comfortable with.

On the other end of the spectrum we have the progressive response of throwing ourselves headlong into trying on new ways of seeing things. This is an attempt to accelerate the cycle of change. It isn't inherently good or bad, but when we're paying Attention we can see it for what it is, rather than choose it as the knee-jerk reaction we're most comfortable with.

There are dangers in both progressive and regressive responses. Neither is right or wrong, worse or better. Neither is even necessarily safer or riskier, even though it often feels safe to do things the way we've always done them. But that's how you drown as the waters rise around your home. The important thing is not to pick a response just because we've always been more comfortable with it. The important thing is to pay Attention, and to recognize our response-ability to try to choose wisely given the situation we're in *now*, in *this* moment in time.

These progressive and regressive responses to an ever-changing reality map pretty closely to two very political words in today's world: liberal and conservative. Conservatives tend to want to slow the cycle of progress, reasoning that the ways we've done things in the past worked well enough to get us to this point, so we shouldn't abandon them with impunity. Liberals, on the other hand, tend to want to speed up the cycle of progress, reasoning that things are far from perfect and that we should experiment with new ways of solving the problems that exist today.

(I am, of course, painting with a very broad brush here. Liberal and conservative viewpoints are complex and polylithic and not locked into any single oversimplified way of viewing things. But, given that I wrote a whole chapter on the fact that reality is infinitely complex you probably already realize that my viewpoint on politics is going to be nuanced.)

The political animosity we have today between people who consider themselves to be conservative and those who consider themselves to be liberal is disturbing, even frightening. Speaking to this conflict is one of the big reasons I decided to write this book. As you can imagine, I don't think the problem is *actually* political in nature. I think it's a problem that's *human* in nature; more specifically, I think it's a failure to pay Attention, and to recognize the larger truth of what we are as human beings.

To talk more about that, let's move on to the next section, where we consider the reasons to pay Attention regarding Big Idea #2—Identity.

————

## REASON #2: SO THAT WE DON'T CONFUSE OUR TOOLS WITH OUR SELVES, THEREBY INJECTING SUFFERING INTO THE WORLD

I sometimes hear human beings referred to as "the tool-using ape." Now, I'm no expert, but my impression is that all apes use tools. So that moniker seems to be a little biased, almost as if people get a kick out of being smarter than apes, which isn't a terribly flattering thought—but one which wouldn't surprise me. Admittedly, though, we are very good at using tools. In fact, we're so good at it that we sometimes don't even notice ourselves doing it—much like a cat doesn't notice itself being a cat.

Tool-using apes we may be, but as we discussed in Big Idea #2, we are also—and perhaps more fundamentally—the conscious awarenesses behind the eyes of those tool-using apes.

When we confuse those two natures, we introduce suffering into the world.

Wait, what? Confuse using a tool with being conscious? Isn't that just as absurd as confusing a saw for your grandmother?

Well, yes. Yes it is. And we also do it all the time. We aren't particularly immune to being absurd, you know. The tragedy is when our absurdity is taken to such extremes that it destroys lives, nations, and species; perhaps even entire ecosystems.

To wrap our heads around this, let's start back from a point we've visited before in this book: suffering.

One of the ways suffering enters the world is through pain. We are, from one perspective, objects moving through space. Sometimes, we smash into things. Other times, it's the objects that smash into us. Anyone who has ever hit their thumb with a hammer knows this well.

And what is a hammer but a tool we use to build things? Tools can cause pain and suffering just as readily as they can be useful. In fact, it may be a feature of reality that anything useful is also dangerous in the wrong context.

Smashing your thumb with a hammer a few times is, from one perspective, simply part of the cost of learning to use a hammer. We can think of the collective suffering of smashed thumbs throughout history as being part of the price of the roofs over our heads today. It's easy to imagine this kind of suffering as being necessary to human progress, and that seems fine for now.

But tools aren't only dangerous while we're learning to use them. They're also dangerous when misused. And not even necessarily like weapons. Sure, a hammer is going to cause a lot of suffering if it's used to smash someone's head in, but I'm talking about something more nuanced than that. Imagine instead trying to use a hammer to pound in a screw. Even if you don't smash your thumb, you'd still do a lot of damage to the screw and the wood, it would take an excruciatingly long time, and it would probably fall apart before too long. That, too, is suffering. Misusing a tool, even if not directly to attack someone, causes destruction, waste, and suffering.

Now, let's bring this full circle. Remember, from Big Idea #2, what our identities are: they are tools we use to interact with other people and the world. But they are tools we often forget about, and are therefore enormously susceptible to misusing. We can also apply this same thinking to specific parts of our identities.

Just a little earlier we were talking about the political conflict between conservatives and liberals, and how I argue that it's not a political problem at all, but rather one of identity. This whole thing about misusing tools is what I mean. Many of the characteristics we think are part of our personalities—part of our identities—are more correctly viewed as tools.

To see how this is the case, we need look no further than the language people use: "I am a liberal." Or, "I am a conservative." Look at that: someone says "I *am* a conservative" in the same breath and with the same certainty as they would say "I *am* a human being."

But clearly that's ridiculous. Clearly what we are as human beings goes deeper than our political leanings. But we're so unpracticed at paying Attention that we can't see what we're doing here.

Conservative and liberal are not things people can be, just like hammers and saws are not things people can be. Liberal and conservative are, rather, *tools for looking at and solving social problems.*

It would be absurd for a carpenter to only ever use a hammer. Carpentry is complex and nuanced, and requires different tools for different situations. A hammer-only carpenter would be a poor carpenter, indeed.

*In exactly the same way*, it is absurd for a human being to only ever use a conservative or liberal lens to look at the world. Human society is complex and nuanced, and requires different tools for different situations. A conservative-only, or a liberal-only human being is a poor citizen, indeed.

We can easily imagine a satire about two feuding carpenters guilds, one that only uses hammers and the other that only uses saws. Meanwhile, the few carpenters who continue to use both are the ones who continue to build and prosper—but only if the warring guilds don't end up burning everything to the ground in their dogmatic, inAttentive frenzy to prove themselves right.

In a moment of politically charged conflict, whether in the halls of a statehouse or across the holiday dinner table, it helps to take a deep breath, pay Attention, and notice what's going on. It's never *actually* about politics. It's about identity—or, more accurately—misidentity. It's about seeing the problem through the lens of the tool you've identified with: the hammerers only see the nails, and the sawyers only see the planks. If, in these moments, you can loosen your death grip on identifying with one tool or the other, then you can be an example to others on how to do the same. When enough of us learn to do this, we will be able to pay Attention together, to more clearly identify the problems we face, and to choose the right tools—hammers or saws, conservative or liberal—to respond to them. When we fail to do this, we cause suffering to perpetuate itself into the future.

In a way, this kind of perpetual suffering is part of the story of human beings—part of our history. I just think it's a story it's past time we try to stop telling. It's been going on for far too long.

The good news is that the beginning of the solution is simple: pay Attention. You can start practicing right now. You don't need equipment, or a teacher, or permission. Everything you need is available to you in this moment, and it only takes a literal minute. Think back on the breathing exercise we did earlier. You can practice with just five breaths. Heck, you can practice with just one breath. All of the excuses we make to avoid starting—things like busyness and forgetfulness—are understandable. But I think, given the increasingly divided and polluted state of things, those excuses are looking weaker every year. The solutions aren't liberal or conservative. The solutions are liberal *and* conservative. Tools are just tools. And if we're going to live up to our self-proclaimed title of "tool-using ape," then we'd better figure this one out, and soon.

The point here is remarkably similar to the previous reason, about holding onto an image of reality that no longer matches actual reality. In the previous section, we saw that when we misapprehend what we perceive in reality, we are more likely to suffer or cause others to suffer. So, we should try our hardest to pay Attention and perceive as accurately as possible. In this second reason, we see that the same thing applies to ourselves: when we more accurately perceive who and what we are, we are less likely to inject suffering into the world by misuse of our tools—many of which aren't even physical objects, but are characteristics or viewpoints our identity uses to make sense of the world. When we can better see and accept ourselves, we can also better see and accept others. So the conclusion is the same: we would do better to always be paying Attention—to be open to seeing who we are.

So how do we begin? What is the force that jars us loose from our excuses? What is it that helps us overcome our fear, laziness, and whatever other excuses we might make to avoid the challenging work of paying Attention in this moment?

What else could it be other than Big Idea #3? It's love, of course—first for ourselves, then for others.

So let's move on now to our third reason to pay Attention, that we may reduce suffering in the world. I think you will find that this one is not just a reason, but also a motivation.

―――――

## REASON #3: SO THAT WE MAY LOVE OURSELVES AND OTHERS WELL

How much time do you spend in negative self-talk? Thinking to yourself, "that was stupid," "why did you do that, you idiot?" "you did a terrible job here," or "you're worthless." It's almost certain that you do it at least sometimes. There are a lot of people who spend countless hours berating themselves like this, day in and day out, the only break from the relentless internal self-criticism being when their head hits the pillow at night.

If you are someone who struggles with negative self-talk (as I myself do, from time to time), I hope Big Idea #3 helped. I hope some part of you can see that you are one more thing the universe created, just as you are; that you don't need to be any specific thing in order to be the culmination of all the moments leading up to this one; and that you've worked ever so hard for so many years to get to this very moment. True, there may not be any fanfare or fireworks or celebration or anything, but that's okay. You're still doing great. I believe it, and I believe you can believe it, too.

We often fill our minds up with noise to crowd something out. Something painful, or something that makes us uncomfortable. Negative self-talk is one of those things. We keep ourselves busy, or play music in the background, or constantly surround ourselves with friends so we don't have to sit alone with our thoughts.

This kind of existence is like being crowded out of our own heads. It's like not being able to see anything but our own self-criticism, our own suffering—or the things we use to distract ourselves from it. It's a pretty dark, lonely, scary place to be. And we wonder, sometimes, if we were to sit alone for a while, if that darkness would cover over us and we would disappear, and no one would notice.

Paying Attention in those times is hard. It feels like watching, frozen, while a monster slowly creeps toward you. And in this case there's no escape, because the monster is in your own head. Your hiding place keeps getting smaller, and smaller, and eventually you're sure you won't have any room left at all, and you'll just vanish from existence without a trace.

How do we find space again inside the tumult of our heads? How do we find our way through the encroaching darkness? The solution is simple (if difficult), and if you've been following along you probably already know what I'm going to say: the solution is to pay Attention, to breathe deeply, to be present, and to recognize that doing these things is not only demonstrating to yourself that you love yourself (and that reality loves you, since you are a part of reality), but also that doing these things reclaims some of the space inside your head.

How does that work?

When you recognize what you are, as we discussed in Big Idea #2—simply a conscious awareness watching from behind the eyes of the human being with your name attached to it—then you can realize that the negative words that are taking up space in your head are not your words, but the words of your identity. They are words you heard in the past, perhaps as a child, that embedded themselves deeply in your mind, and now they play as if on a loop, over and over across your days. They are much like one of your physical scars—a wound you received at some point that has healed, somewhat, but still might give an irritating twinge now and then.

The difference between your physical scars and your mental/emotional ones is that we learn to recognize our physical ones as we watch the wounds they used to be heal. Whereas we make the mistake of thinking our mental/emotional scars are *who we are*. Of course our scars are *part* of who we are—part of our identity. But they are not who we are. Who we are is beyond things like physical, mental, or emotional damage. We are just the Observer, the awareness, and we can have infinite compassion for the little, beautiful human identity whose eyes we look out of every moment of their lives.

When you hear that negative self-talk, don't drown it out or argue with it. Instead, take a deep breath, pay Attention to the moment, and recognize the words for what they are—just an echo of the past. They aren't true. They are simply one perspective-based story your identity is clinging to. Every time you pay Attention and recognize this, you take some of the strength away from those thoughts. You heal the wound a little more, and eventually the thoughts will hardly bother you anymore.

When you feel alone, don't always rush to fill that void with socializing or conversation. Instead, take a deep breath, pay Attention to the moment, and allow yourself to notice that you are as safe as you have ever been. That every moment of your life you have negotiated well enough to bring you to this moment, and that there couldn't be more evidence that you're doing an amazing job of being human. The encroaching darkness you sense may be real, but it isn't an enemy. It's a part of you, and it's trying to teach you something, to help you learn to care for yourself. Yes, sometimes lessons are painful. But pain is part of life, and it hasn't killed us so far. The way to minimize pain is by getting through it. When we resist the pain, or thrash around, we hurt ourselves more. But when we are present and pay Attention, and sit with the pain, we can learn what it has to teach us.

Life will inevitably be full of pain. We are all just little objects moving through a big space. We will bump into things, both physical, mental, and emotional, and those things will damage us. You've experienced it, I've experienced it, and when we acknowledge our shared experience we are empowered to have compassion for one another and for everyone and everything else who suffers as we do.

It is not the minimizing of pain which is the goal of life. Pain is, and will be. The goal of life is to be alive, and to try to learn, and pain is—though it seems terribly unfair—one of our greatest teachers. We learn best when we pay Attention, and so we must also try our best to pay Attention to our mental and emotional wounds. Not only will we learn what they have to teach us, but we will be better able to keep them clean so that they may heal.

This is hard work. Perhaps the hardest. Loving yourself in this way can be scary and exhausting. But there is, once again, the consolation of the evidence that you already love yourself. How do I know this? Because you're here. You're reading these words. You argue with the negative self-talk, which means there's a fierce little part of you that wants you to be big and beautiful and successful and healthy. You reach out to others in times of despair, which means there's a feisty part of you that wants to rail against the darkness, to beat it back with torches, to laugh and play and dance while you're here. That part of you deserves to express itself just as much as the rest. It knows it, and it's just waiting for you to recognize it, too. How else could you do so but by paying it some Attention?

We love ourselves well when we do our best to pay Attention to all the different parts of ourselves. None are better or more deserving. Each of them makes us who we are. The fact that we had to learn, as children, which of them to suppress in order to fit into the rules and regulations of our family and our upbringing doesn't mean that we are bad, or unworthy, or deserve whatever suffering we put ourselves through. No, we deserve love. And we can give ourselves love. We don't need anyone's permission. We don't need anyone's blessing. We don't need anyone's help. Everything we need to love ourselves is already present inside us, in this very moment. All we need to do in order to see it is pay Attention.

Of course, while it's true that we don't need anyone's permission, you have mine: go and love yourself.

And while it's true that we don't need anyone's blessing, you have mine: may you be aware of the fullness of your love for yourself!

And while it's true that we don't need anyone's help, you have mine: it is why I've written this book, and if I've written others since this one was published, I'm sure it's also why I wrote them.

I am far from perfect, and my love is a small thing, like my tiny human self. Still, for what little it's worth, you also have my love.

I am far from perfect, and thus I don't really think anyone should listen to me, but I also believe that you ought to decide for yourself what you believe, and how you should be.

I am far from perfect, and thus am uncomfortable thinking that I might be an example to others, but one lesson I seem to have learned well is to love myself. I don't often struggle with negative self-talk, and I find a great deal of spaciousness inside my head. I am much more curious than self-critical, and I love being the way I am. I hope you can love being the way you are, too. You deserve all the space you can create for yourself in the one place in which you have total freedom: inside your own experience of being.

So the point of this third reason to pay Attention is so that you can learn to see and accept yourself as you are. Loving yourself in this way gives you all the space you need. And as a bonus, it allows you to love others in the same way, giving them all the space they need.

It's easy to dismiss all the platitudinous statements about love as woo-woo, wishy-washy, touchy-feely, or hippie-dippie, or whatever other hyphenated adjectives you use to indicate when something is "out there." But when we think of love as being the universal force causing effort to be directed, as Big Idea #3 suggests, they do make a consistent and persuasive kind of sense.

"Love makes the world go 'round."

"All you need is love."

"Love will find a way."

These statements may not be true in the actual sense of how the universe works, but I hope I've made it clear that I think nothing we're capable of thinking is true in the actual sense of how the universe works. We don't know anything. And if this idea about love is enough to move us as individuals and us as humanity forward into the future, then why should we argue with it? It is a lesson I hope we all learn, again and again, on and on into the future so distant it is no longer imaginable.

All these reasons to pay Attention, and all the other reasons we haven't discussed, are aimed at a single goal: to help you be, in this moment, at peace and full of love, so that you may be, in every moment to come, at peace and full of love, so that you may help others be at peace and full of love. And when the moment of your human life's end arrives—the moment of your death—that you embrace it with the same serenity, curiosity, joyfulness, and gratitude that has suffused every moment of your life leading up to it. This is what makes a life good; this is what makes up the

Good Life. Simply being here, in this moment, paying Attention, accepting that what is, is, and trying to discern and describe it to others as best you can.

Of course this is an absurd and impossible goal. Learning to be human is impossible, because we're never done with it. We're always continuing to learn, to grow. We're always becoming something new, always in the process of, in this very moment, transforming into the future version of ourselves.

Learning anything is hard. It requires you to fail, again and again, and every time you fail, to try again. How much harder is it, then, to learn to be human: the one thing that enables you to learn everything else? I urge you not to become discouraged at the difficulty of the task—even though I know you will become discouraged. It's okay. I get discouraged, too. No one ever learned anything without making some mistakes. The good news is that, since there's no way to avoid making them, we might as well forgive ourselves and each other when we do, so that we can get back to trying again with a minimum of fuss.

And when we catch a glimpse of how absurd it all is, all this trying and failing and trying again, with nothing but the promise of continued trying and failing, what else can we do but laugh? Or cry. Or hold someone we love tight, sharing the pain and the joy with them. There is something beautiful in the futility of it all, something that can't quite be expressed in words, or emotions, or equations, or any of our other tools for understanding reality. But that doesn't mean those words, or emotions, or equations are insufficient. Because they are a part of us just as surely as my experience of writing these words, and your experience of reading them right now. That, I think, is worth celebrating. Worth embracing. Worth paying Attention to. Worth living, and loving. And even, I suppose, though it can be ever so difficult to see, worth dying for.

And the thing I wonder most of all is what the world would look like if it was made up of enough people who recognized what truth is, who knew themselves for who and what they are, who love themselves well and so love their neighbors well, and who contribute little or nothing to the collective suffering of all —who, in fact, contribute their time and effort to the alleviation of suffering. What would that world look like?

The forest is made up of the trees, yes. And we are like the trees, not the forest. But we cannot change the forest—only ourselves. So when we recognize that, with a change of perspective, the distinction between the forest and the tree is closer to meaningless than our thinker thought, we can, with love, get to work on being the best version of ourself we can be. And the more healthy trees we have, the healthier the forest of life on this planet will be.

Well, this is the end. What do you think of this journey we've been on together? What has it been like for you? What have you learned? Noticed? Payed Attention to? Take a moment to reflect.

If you like, feel free to send me your thoughts. I would welcome seeing them in my inbox, and I'll do my best to reply. You can reach me at mm@michaelmarvosh.com.

I'm grateful, you know. Grateful for having finished this book, certainly (it was one of the hardest things I've done so far), but more grateful to you for having read it. Thank you.

I would like to make one small request of you. If this has helped you in some way, whether by giving you a new way of looking at the world or your life, or by helping you see the importance of paying Attention, or even in some way I may not have intended and didn't anticipate, then please consider sharing the book with someone you know who might similarly benefit from it. I would be honored if you were to recommend it or—if you're feeling particularly generous—gift a second copy.

I ask this because I truly believe the ideas in this book are important, but challenging. They won't spread unless we all do the work of trying to spread them. I wrote this book because there was something I needed to say. I would be honored and grateful if you were to help me say it.

And last, a blessing:

If there is such a thing as truth, may you discover it.

If there is such a thing as peace, may you know it.

If there is such a thing as love, may you feel it.

I believe in these things,

And I am confident that,

If you seek

in earnest, with Attention,

You will find.

# APPENDIX

(YOU KNOW, THE PART THAT MIGHT BE
USEFUL AND HAVE A FUNCTION, BUT
WHICH YOU CAN USUALLY CUT OUT
WITHOUT ANY ILL-EFFECT.)

## HOW TO PAY ATTENTION

From early on in the process of writing this book I have struggled with genre. Whenever I talked to other writers or sought out information about how to classify the book, one genre kept coming up: self-help.

I hated it. I didn't want to write a self-help book. Self-help books are all about embracing the narrative. About telling yourself a story about how great you are, or how deserving, or how clever, or how popular, or whatever. They always seemed to me to be trying to make the legitimately difficult practice of being human look easier than it actually is. They were, in other words, much too fluffy for me.

I wanted to write a book about something rock solid: the truth. About how we don't know anything, and our stories are ever so limited, and it is our attachment to them that's the problem, the thing that causes all our suffering. This stuff isn't about meeting that perfect person, or making a bunch of money, or whatever other distraction people are looking for to help them forget, for a while, about how genuinely difficult life is. (Not that there's anything wrong with forgetting—it, too, is part of what makes us human. It's just not what I wanted to talk about.)

Well, I don't know if I succeeded. Maybe this book does read "self-help" on the back cover. I guess it doesn't matter. I guess I need to make my peace with whatever comes, if I'm going to take my own medicine. It's funny, isn't it, how we inevitably get caught up in our own little dramas, even when we're entirely aware that they're nothing but dramas? How very... human of me.

In any case, up to this point in the book I've tried to make it mostly about ways of looking at things, rather than about story-telling. I realize that this was an exercise in futility, because we can't *think* without perspective-based narrative, but still: I wanted to strip things down as close as possible to the *looking*, the *perceiving*, the *noticing*, because those are all so closely related to my conclusion that we should *pay Attention*.

But I ran into this challenge, which is that I imagined that you, my reader, might end up, after all the words up to this point, with this question: "but *how* do I pay Attention?"

The question always felt a little strange to me. I didn't actually know if I should answer it. Even as I write this, I'm not sure it's the right decision to include it in the book. But, well... there's no such thing as a right decision, just ones that work out or not, and we can learn from both outcomes. So I might as well do my best here.

The reason the question feels strange to me, as best I can figure, is that asking how to pay Attention seems a bit like asking how to use your hand. I can't *tell* you how to use your hand. Sure, I can *show* you how I use *my* hand. But the only way anyone ever learned how to use their hand is by using it. We don't remember learning how to use our hands because we were babies when we did it, but it stands to reason that each of us spent many, many hours *practicing* how to use our hands.

It's the same thing with Attention. You have to practice. You can't be taught *how* to do it, because you already *know* how to do it. It's simply a matter of *doing it* more, and noticing what it's like, and getting more comfortable with it, until it's as easy as using your hand (honestly I don't know if it ever gets that easy, but I like to hope it does).

So, in that spirit, I will surrender and engage in a little bit of self-help writing. Below are a few exercises I do to practice paying Attention. (And keep in mind that I am far from the greatest expert on the practice.)

But, no matter what you do, try to remember that there are no shortcuts here. This is not down to how clever you are, or how good you were in school, or how many sports you played, or how popular you are. This is about *being human*, a thing to which we are all equally suited for and inexperienced at—depending on how you look at it. You will certainly fail, in the same way you skinned your knees a few times while learning to ride a bike, in the same way you had some embarrassing breakups, in the same way, even, that you still trip over your own feet sometimes and hope no one notices. Keep in mind that failure is just feedback that you're drifting off the path. As long as you keep going, well... you're still going. And that's all any of us can do: keep going. (Oh, and love yourself. Which, as I've already argued, I think you already do, even if you don't let yourself notice.)

Anyway, with that, here are my three favorite exercises for practicing paying Attention:

————

## 1. Meditation

Meditation can be difficult to understand, and even a little off-putting sometimes. In the hopes of alleviating whatever qualms you may have along those lines, I'll try to describe how I look at this exercise.

First, since we are practicing paying Attention, I am not

talking about what's usually called Transcendental Meditation (or TM). I'm not sure I myself understand TM, but it seems to have to do with trying to access "higher" states of consciousness. My biggest problem here is that, since I'm not particularly confident that higher states of consciousness exist, I'm not very willing to spend a bunch of time trying to access them. If I stumble across one someday, I hope I'll be able to pay Attention and learn something, but for now, TM is quite a long way outside my own personal experience of existence.

No, I'm talking specifically about what is often called "mindfulness meditation," a term I don't prefer for previously mentioned reasons: I'd rather talk about paying Attention than about being mindful, because I don't think it necessarily has anything to do with our minds.

All I mean when I talk about meditating is trying, for some period of time, to minimize all physical and mental activity *other* than paying Attention. You can meditate for a few seconds, several minutes, a couple hours, or for the rest of your life. There are no rules to this. It's just trying to practice paying Attention, noticing when your mind wanders to the past or the future or some other train of thought, and bringing it back to the wordless experience of the present moment.

A lot of people seem to think that meditation is about trying to *not think*. But I think this is a misunderstanding—though it is an understandable misunderstanding. We can easily see why someone might imagine they need to try to not think: it's because all day, every day, they find themselves thinking. There is an incessant chatter filling their awareness. So they think that's just the way they are. But this nonstop internal narrative isn't the default way human beings operate. It's simply a learned behavior, exactly the same as drumming your fingers on the table. If you were in the habit of constantly drumming your fingers, it would be challenging for you to sit with your hands still for an hour. It would take a lot of effort, and a lot of Attention. Meditation is exactly the same kind of thing, but for your thoughts instead of your fingers.

So, how does one meditate? Well, there's no single right answer to the question. You should experiment for yourself. But one easy place to start is by doing an exercise very similar to the one we did at the beginning of the last chapter of the book, on paying Attention. Simply find a safe, quiet place to sit, and focus the entirety of your Attention on your breathing for five slow, measured breaths. If you notice your thoughts wandering (and you will), don't get upset, just be aware of it, and let them go. Basically, you're giving yourself a redo. Five breaths, redo if needed. When you feel ready, you can bump it up to ten breaths. Eventually you'll get to the point where you lose count—either because your thoughts wandered and you need a redo, or because your Attention is fixed on your breath so well that there's no room to remember your numbers. In either case, that's fine.

By doing this exercise in a calm, quiet space, you're preparing yourself to try to do it in more and more complicated, noisy environments. Try it while watching a movie. Try it while taking a shower. Try it while eating a meal. Try it while having a conversation (it's very difficult to do while also having to talk). Try it while your kids are having a tantrum (and you thought the conversation one was hard).

The outcome of getting really good at paying Attention in this way is that we can more easily see that, in every situation, our Observer is safe. Even if our physical body is in a precarious place and is grasping for our Attention, we can try to maintain the perspective, which is always true, that we are simply the one watching the movie of our lives unfold. This kind of Attention is, I think, also the goal of martial arts, for example. Like in those slow-motion scenes in the movies: that we can simultaneously be *in* an experience, and also *above* it, Observing it.

The other outcome of a meditation practice is that you get a ton of experience with giving yourself a redo. When you meditate, your thoughts inevitably intrude. That's okay, start over. Redo. Thirty seconds later (or ten seconds) the same thing happens again. Take a breath. Redo. Over and over. It might happen two dozen times during a single meditation session. Don't get upset, just give yourself a redo. As you get better and better at practicing that skill in meditation, you'll get better and better at practicing that skill in life. Lost your temper with someone? Redo. Slipped into some negative self-talk? Redo. Messed up on a big project? Redo. That's all life is, really, is a long series of attempts to do things. Of course you'll make mistakes; that's how we learn not to make mistakes. Don't get upset, just take a redo.

And the starting point for learning these incredibly difficult skills is the same as the starting point for learning any incredibly difficult skill: start with the simplest expression of it. Start with one breath.

That's what meditation is for. If it interests you, give it a try. Everything you need to start is available to you right this moment.

---

## 2. Yoga

If meditation is difficult or distasteful for you, it's possible that you need something for your body to do while your mind focuses. For me, yoga can help solve that problem.

There are many kinds of yoga, because there are many reasons people do yoga. Some people do it as strength training. Some people do it to increase flexibility. Some people do it for the social aspect. Some people do it because they like pain, I guess. (I did hot yoga once, and it is literally the worst I can ever remember feeling.)

I do yoga once or twice a week to practice paying Attention. I think it's a very effective tool for this.

If you want to try it, I suggest a beginner's class, or some kind of slow flow (flow being the word yogis use to describe moving between poses). The class I attend is called "gentle yoga."

At first, yoga probably won't be great for practicing paying Attention. I remember when I started practicing yoga several years ago, a lot of my attention was taken up by watching the instructor and trying to figure out how I was supposed to place my body. But after a while, as I got familiar with the poses, I stopped worrying about whether I was doing them "right," and just started paying Attention to what I was feeling in my body. Now the poses and the way my body fits into them serve as information in the moment for me to pay Attention to. No need to think. I can just be present in the moment. As a bonus, yoga poses are always synchronized to the breath, so I also get to practice the same kind of breath-awareness that I practice while meditating. That's what yoga is like: moving meditation.

In fact, any kind of safe, calm, repetitive movement can be an excellent tool for practicing paying Attention. Hiking or jogging are also excellent ways to get out of your head and into your body—into your breath.

And, speaking of getting out of your head and into your body by using your breath, we have our third exercise...

————

### 3. Wim Hof

I recently learned this breathing exercise, and it quickly impressed me as one of the quickest and most effective tools I'd ever encountered for getting out of my head and into my body. It's almost shocking, in a way. Quite literally. But in a healthy way.

Wim Hof is a Dutch man who discovered he could use this breathing technique to prepare his body to do extreme activities like submerge himself in ice-cold water for hours at a time, swim for hundreds of meters below the surface of a frozen lake, or climb Mount Everest wearing nothing but shorts.

I have no such interest in those kinds of activities, but Hof's breathing technique is still an incredibly useful tool for activating the body—almost jump-starting it—which can be immensely helpful in shocking yourself out of an endless loop of thinking about the past or future or whatever. When your body feels awake and alive and is screaming at you that it's ready to go *do something*, it's impossible to ignore, and very difficult to avoid paying Attention to the present moment. You can use that energy to meditate, or exercise, or enter into a deep state of relaxation before you go to sleep. You could do almost anything with it.

You can probably find better explanations of the Wim Hof breathing technique online, but I'll briefly explain it here.

Lie flat on the ground or sit up straight in a chair (so you can breathe deeply unhindered). The first part of the technique is to breathe very deeply and rather quickly 30-35 times. This hyper-oxygenates your blood (and subsequently all your cells), so that when you move onto the next part of the technique your body is highly stimulated and energized, ready to leap into whatever action you demand of it. You can easily feel the effects of this breathing. They're quite strong, though for me they are slightly different each time I do the technique. Sometimes I feel my whole body tingling. Sometimes I feel a strong pulsating in my hands and feet. Sometimes I feel warm, sometimes cold. There's no predicting it, only trusting that oxygen is good for me, and my body knows what to do with the wealth of it I'm delivering.

The next part of the technique is that, immediately following your last deep breath, you squeeze all the air out of your lungs, and then hold that out-breath for as long as you can, while trying to relax your body and slow your heart rate (you should be able to feel your heart pounding). You'll almost certainly surprise yourself with how long you can go. The first time I did the technique, I remember there were definitely some panicky half-attempts to breathe in. My heart was racing because I was unfamiliar with the feeling, and each time my brain told me I needed to breathe, I twitched with the effort of calming it down and assuring it that we had plenty of oxygen already. It may take you a time or two to become familiar with the feeling, but soon you should be able to hold this out-breath for a minute, 90 seconds, two minutes, or even more! In my experience, the time seems to go by very quickly. I'm always surprised when my timer reaches two minutes. Of course, the exact duration doesn't matter. The point is to hold this out-breath for as long as you can, relaxing and calming your mind and body, overcoming your brain's normal programming.

After the amount of time passes, or once you absolutely can't hold it anymore, you take a single, deep breath, filling your lungs, and hold that as well, for 15 or 20 seconds. Pay attention to the feelings in your body. I've experienced everything from lightheaded euphoria to seemingly endless wells of calm energy.

After holding this one big breath for 15 to 20 seconds, begin again, and repeat the whole exercise. Breathe in, breathe out, 30 times quickly. Push all the air out. Relax your whole body, slow your heart down, and pay attention to the gap between what your brain tells you you need to do and what your body is demonstrably capable of doing. Try to push 10 seconds past how long you think you can go. When you can't wait any longer, take a single, deep breath, filling your lungs. Hold it for 15 to 20 seconds. Then begin again.

You should do the exercise at least three times. You'll notice it change each time as you pump more and more oxygen into your cells. Three times is a nice arc of experience, but you can do more if you like. As many as six repetitions in a single sitting is fine for a beginner, but probably not more. Let your body tell you when it's had enough between those three and six repetitions.

Now, perhaps you've already set the book down and spent 10 minutes doing the Wim Hof breathing exercise. If so, great. I hope you had an experience worth remembering, and I hope that experience gives you some ideas about how you might be able to better pay Attention over the next few days, weeks, or months.

So that's it. That's all the how-to I have for you. You can meditate or do Wim Hof just about literally anytime. You're entirely self-equipped for those exercises, just as you are for paying Attention, for loving yourself, and for existing in this moment.

# ACKNOWLEDGMENTS

As I mentioned a couple times in the text itself, writing a book is *hard*. As I've reflected on it, though, and paid Attention during the process, I've also come to realize that it's also quite easy. Like so many things, it all depends on the perspective you take.

Writing a book is hard in the way working through conflict with a friend or family member is hard. It's time-consuming, emotional, draining, crazymaking. You argue with and doubt yourself, yet still hurl yourself back into it again and again.

But it's easy, too, like hanging out with that same friend or family member. It gets comfortable, relaxing even. There's an immediacy to the process, a "now-ness," that feels quite remarkable. Eventually I got to a finished product which, though not perfect, was the best I could do. The book became more like a relationship I'd developed than a thing I'd produced.

I want to first acknowledge, appreciate, and celebrate the people who helped bring me, Michael Marvosh, to this relationship.

First, of course, is my family. My parents, Dave and Suzanne Marvosh, created what sadly seems like a rarity these days: a mostly functional family. Emily and Andrew, my brother and sister, were always there with me through the crucible of childhood. What an immense help siblings can be to one another. Like the book, none of us are perfect. But all of us are doing our best. I love all four of you more than I can say. Thank you for helping me grow.

Next comes my wife, Marissa. Thank you for believing in me,

and for trying to understand me, even when I don't understand myself. I couldn't ask for a better partner in life.

Though they are all gone now, my grandparents, too, played a crucial role in shaping who I am today. Grandma and Grandad were always loving and welcoming, and Grandpa Nick, who lived next door to us until we moved when I was seven or eight, showed me how to work hard, love nature, be curious, and laugh freely.

Eric Cannedy, my best friend in college and in my first few years moving to a new state, helped teach me how to love, how to work through tough times, how to hold onto important relationships (many of which up to that point in my life I'd too-easily walked away from). I am often sad that he is gone, and I am forever grateful for his love and friendship.

Mary Makarios compassionately coached me through my emotional rebirth. She knew about—and encouraged—the kernel of the idea for this book before anyone else.

My fellow seekers and coaches from the School of Lost Borders. Those twelve days in the desert cracked me open and showed me my tender yet strong heart. I will be forever grateful for your loving help.

All my other friends and family members also deserve mention here. You are always in my thoughts, and I am sorry I cannot name you all.

Then there is the army of people who helped bring this book to the relationship.

My editor, Gillian Hill, understood the complexity and ambiguity of my topic, yet nonetheless enthusiastically waded into it with me. My proofreader, Holly Beech, who in addition to her wonderfully critical eye had so many kind words to say (and generously wrote the back cover text). My designer, Nathan Warner, who looks at the world so differently than I, gently coaxed me into seeing things from his oh-so important aesthetic perspective. Finally, Stacey Smekofske helped coach me through the nitpicky details of self publishing.

In addition, there are those who were kind enough to read early (very rough) drafts of the book: Brian Roemen and Sam Johnson (also good friends of mine), Will Newton, and Soren Teeple. Thank you all.

My friends in The Hybrid Society, Sean Mabry, Ay Mey Lie, and Leslie Holt, were there when I decided to pivot from some freelancing nonsense to writing a book. You are all remarkable people, and I am so excited to see the work you continue to bring to the world. Thank you for your support. Similarly, my writing group the Tortoises, including Alexa Hulsey, Areanne Lloyd, and Deborah Graham: thank you for your steadiness and encouragement, and for working just as diligently as me (if not moreso).

Shane Johnson was kind and generous to let me use his recording studio to record the audiobook. Trevor Kraus, though we didn't end up working together, generously gave me a great deal of time and attention on an earlier draft of the book. And Brannan Sirratt, though we only spoke briefly, helped show me how incredibly talented people can spread their work through the world. Thank you all.

Stephen Warley, of Life Skills that Matter, met me early in my journey, and believed in me long before I learned how to believe in myself. Thank you, Stephen, for teaching me. You make a difference in a lot of people's lives.

Lastly, two men who don't know me but who have had an outsized impact in shaping who I have become. Sean McCabe deserves thanks for helping me develop my writing habit. It came slowly, and ungratefully on my part, and I still don't do it exactly the way he recommended. But, if not for him, I wouldn't have learned to do it my own way. Finally, I want to thank Seth Godin for his work. For years his writing has been feeding my courage, and this book wouldn't exist without it. Thank you, Seth.

# AUTHOR BIO

Michael Marvosh guesses that he's supposed to write this author bio thing in the third person. He wonders why that is. To create the perception of an additional layer of separation between him and you, his reader? Or to make it somehow more inviting for you, if you're reading this bio prior to having read the book?

Well... do you feel invited?

If you pay Attention, these few sentences will have told you all you need to know about Michael. He is incessantly curious, and has been for as long as he can remember. He has few qualms about asking impertinent questions—and is hard at work losing the ones that remain. After decades of questioning, Michael thinks he's found a handful of solid answers, and he simply needed to share them with you. That's where this book came from. And, he hopes, many books yet to come.

Michael lives in Boise, Idaho, with his family.